Straight and N

A comedy

Jimmie Chinn

Samuel French - London
New York - Toronto - Hollywood

Please see page iv for further copyright information.

for PETER

STRAIGHT AND NARROW

First presented by Theatre West Four in October 1987
with the following cast of characters:

Bob	Peter Rose
Jeff	Mick Cawson
Nona	Pat Nicholls
Lois	Debbie Ardrey
Vera	Betty Price
Bill	Tim Webster
Arthur	Brian Aldred

Directed by Joanne Burnett

The play was subsequently presented at the Duke's Head
Theatre, Richmond, Surrey, in May 1989 with the following cast:

Bob	David Gillies
Jeff	George Phillips
Nona	Wendy MacAdam
Lois	Sally Campbell
Vera	Helen Barnaby
Bill	Peter Dawson
Arthur	Noël Hill

Directed by David Gillies

It was presented by Linnit Productions Ltd and Allan
Davis Ltd at Wyndham's Theatre, London, on 18th
March 1992 with the following cast:

Bob	Nicholas Lyndhurst
Jeff	Neil Daglish
Nona	Anna Keaveney
Lois	Melanie Kilburn
Vera	Carmel McSharry
Bill	Peter Jonfield
Arthur	John Hartley

Directed by Allan Davis
Designed by Carl Toms
Lighting by Kevin Sleep

CHARACTERS

Bob
Jeff
Nona
Lois
Vera
Bill
Arthur

The play takes place in the home of Bob and Jeff, just outside Manchester

Time—a Saturday afternoon in July, not so long ago

Other plays by Jimmie Chinn
published by Samuel French Ltd

But Yesterday
From Here to the Library
In Room Five Hundred and Four
Interior Designs
Pity About Kitty
A Respectable Funeral
Take Away the Lady
Too Long an Autumn

ACT I

The lounge/sitting-room of Bob's and Jeff's semi-detached somewhere on the outskirts of Manchester. A Saturday afternoon in July, not so long ago

The set should be skeletal, suggesting two rooms which have been knocked into one. At the back (once a narrow passageway/hall) we can see the stairs leading up to the bedrooms, etc. Unseen is the street door and also unseen is the door to the kitchen. On one wall of the room are patio doors leading to a small back garden; in the opposite wall maybe a bay window overlooking the street. The fireplace, we assume, is in the fourth wall, above which is "The Picture". Other paintings by Bob hang in the room. There must be a space, on either side, downstage of the set for an entrance and exit. There is a small table with a telephone and answering-machine. The room is tastefully furnished, modern but cosy and comfortable rather than elegant

The CURTAIN *rises in darkness and we hear Vera singing "Home, Sweet Home". A light comes up to reveal Bob,* DL, *on the telephone, his back to us*

Bob (*ending the call into the phone*) We'd love to—but we can't . . . sorry. (*He replaces the receiver and turns to the audience. Alone in his light*) The trouble is—nothing's simple in life, is it? I mean, nothing's simple. The most ordinary, everyday, humdrum little things can turn out to be so complicated—no? And everybody tells lies, have you noticed? I don't mean great huge whopping lies—the sort real liars tell—but the inoffensive little lies we all tell to get out of ordinary awkward situations. (*He crosses to* C) I mean, why can't we just say "no" when that extremely boring friend asks us round to dinner? "No, I'm sorry, I can't come—I don't want to come!" Why can't we just say it? But we don't, do we? We either say, "Oh, how lovely, I'd adore to come", and hope he drops dead before the appointed day then we can say, "Oh, would you believe—and there was I due to go to dinner on Friday!"

It's always a Friday, have you noticed? It's because they've something better to do on Saturday, and Sunday they have to work the next day.

Or we make an excuse, don't we? Another lie of course. "Oh, would you believe—we're due at Fred and Joan's that night—what a pity!" And what do they do? Change the bloody date to catch you out!

And the stuff they give you to eat—have you noticed? God help us. And you don't eat all day just to make sure you're simply bloody ravenous by the time you get there. And you know, don't you, as soon as you enter the door? You can smell it. Wafting across the hall from the kitchen.

You see, I like my food simple. Chops and things. Roast beef and Yorkshire, gravy and peas; lamb with mint sauce or pork with crackling;

steak, well done with chips . . . stuff you can actually eat! And everything separate on the plate. I hate a mess, don't you? A congealed mass—cooked three weeks ago, kept in a freezer and warmed in a microwave for two minutes. (*He pulls a face*) Yuukk!

And you sit round that table and chat—small talk while she keeps nipping to the kitchen smiling and saying, "It's only simple—nothing fancy—a recipe I got in Venezuela!" And your heart sinks, doesn't it? I long to cry out, "If it's filth I'm sodding off home!" But you don't, do you? We all tell lies again. "Smells delicious, love." Then it arrives, after the avocado with gunge, and there it sits—a huge earthenware dish containing God knows what—and she takes the lid off—and it's pink! Pink! With brown bits floating menacingly on top. And we all look at it. And what do we say? "How wonderful, Margo—what is it?" And I long to cry out: "Don't tell us—for God's sake don't tell us!"

But she does, doesn't she? She goes through every detail and says that it's best left sixteen weeks before it's eaten and that the mouldy bits are a real delicacy in Mozambique . . . and we all tell lies! (*He moves* DL)

I mean, at Sunday School they always said, "Tell the truth and shame the devil", but you can't, can you? It upsets too many people. So you sit there, forcing this stuff down your throat hoping the pudding's going to be chocolate sponge with chocolate sauce . . . but it never is.

More lights start to come up on the room

Jeff enters from the hall. He is dressed in running shorts and vest and is breathless and sweating from running. He goes into the kitchen. He comes back from the kitchen with a can of drink

Bob watches him for a while

(*To the audience*) He'll eat anything. He will. Anything. "As long as it's healthy." He's marvellous. My Auntie Trish used to say, about my Uncle Cedric that is, "He'd eat kippers and custard if I gave it to him!"

Jeff, exhausted, flops down on the sofa

(*Still to the audience*) Take no notice. He's been jogging or whatever they call it. And mark my words, he'll kill his soddin' self before he's much older. He likes to pretend he's fit. Fit, I ask you! Stubs his toe and he's in bed a fortnight!

He smiles at us warmly

I'm Bob. Robert Swift. Robert Henry Samuel Swift actually—but I don't tell everybody—and you can call me Bob.

Jeff (*unaware of the audience*) Jesus, I'm knackered!

Bob (*to the audience*) What did I tell you? That's Jeff. Jeffrey Shotter. He's only got the one name, and actually between you and me, he's lucky to have that—and you can call him anything you like!

"Shotter and Swift". Sounds like a double act, doesn't it? And, to tell the truth, we are a double-act . . . in more ways than one. For a start, we run a business together. "KITCHENS". That's right—kitchens. We design them, fit them, everything in fact. We've been at it for years. He's a plumber by trade and I'm a joiner—carpenter—call it what you will. Plus, I have an artistic side to my nature. I went to tap and ballet till I was nine, see—hence why I'm good at the designing side of the work. (*He goes to Jeff*)

Jeff What's for tea? I'm starving.

Bob "Kippers and custard and see if you like it!"

Jeff (*not listening, rising to go*) What time? (*He takes an apple from a bowl on the table*)

Bob Half an hour.

Jeff exits, upstairs

More lights come up and the room grows warm with afternoon sunshine. Bob walks about the room showing it off

Jeff and I have been partners now for yonks, and this is our lounge—living-room—call it what you like. This is our couch, and our carpet; our tables and chairs, and these are my paintings—I mean I did them—good, aren't they? Actually, it's just like a real house, isn't it? Tell you the truth, we have a friend called Marion who was heard to whisper, "they've got a double bed—just like a real couple!" She did. Funny, isn't it? Women can be like that, can't they? You know, part of my trouble is: I've always been surrounded by women. My mum—Vera—what else? You'll meet her later on. My two sisters: Nona, she's the eldest, and Lois, she's married to Bill. He's lovely—I hope you'll like him . . . (*He leans against the* R *proscenium*)

Nona enters from the hall, carrying shopping

Nona (*calling off*) I'm through here in the lounge, Lois. (*To herself*) God, it's sweltering in here. (*She puts the shopping on the sideboard and opens the patio doors which lead out into the garden*)

Bob That's Nona, she's older than me, married to Arthur—but don't mention him whatever you do. (*Lowering his voice*) He's gone off with a younger woman—Brenda Brierley who works in Boots!

Nona (*obviously unaware of Bob's presence*) It's like an oven in here, Lois.

Lois appears

Lois Hey, Nona, this key's stuck in the lock—I can't shift it.

Nona (*calling*) You have to twist twice—give it a shove—then pull. It's supposed to be burglar-proof. (*She goes around the room watering plants*)

Lois exits

Bob I should mention by the way—Nona's very highly strung, which has got worse since he went off with "you-know-who".

Nona (*to herself, slightly dizzy*) I'm all light-headed here. I think I'm going through the change.

Bob That's not true—Nona went through the change when she was sixteen and she's never been the same since.

Lois enters carrying more shopping. She is slightly younger than Nona and is rather heavily pregnant

Lois (*entering*) What a funny front door, Nona. I'm sure I've wrenched my shoulder.

Nona (*on her hands and knees waving a box of Go-Cat*) Puss-puss—here, kitty-kitty . . .

Lois What are you doing, Nona?

Nona What d'you mean, what am I doing? What does it look like I'm doing? I'm looking for the cat. He's usually sitting right here. (*She looks for the cat*)

Bob (*to the audience*) Oh, yes, we have a cat. Butch. But he isn't—we've had the poor bugger done!

Lois (*putting down her shopping on the sofa table*) Oh, leave it. I don't like cats—I never did.

Nona (*worried*) It's all right for you to say leave it—while they're away, that cat's my responsibility, Lois.

Lois (*looking about the room*) Hey, they've had it beautified, haven't they? Done up.

Nona It's been redecorated for weeks.

Lois Well I haven't been for weeks, have I? The last time I came it was brown, wasn't it?

Nona Course it wasn't brown, Lois. It's never been brown.

Lois Well, it wasn't this colour.

Bob (*to the audience*) Actually, it was *café au lait*.

Lois Well, I don't dislike it I suppose. I expect they've nothing better to do than keep decorating. (*Sitting on the sofa*) God, I must sit down—I'm exhausted.

Nona You should get your weight down, kid. I looked at you in Marks. Like the side of a bloody house.

Lois (*pretending to be offended*) Thank you! I am several months pregnant, Nona.

Nona All the more reason why you should watch what you're eating. It can bring on your heart can that.

Bob (*to the audience*) Nona's inherited my mum's optimism—she always looks on the bright side.

Nona (*still concerned about the cat*) Pussy-pussy . . . Come to Auntie Nona. (*She looks for the cat near the windows*)

Lois Oh, for God's sake leave it. It's probably dead down by the rhubarb.

Nona (*lacking Lois's humour*) They haven't got any rhubarb.

Lois (*inspecting her feet*) Here, look, are my ankles swelling?

Nona You're swelling all over—are you sure it's right? (*She stands near Lois*)

Lois I'm having a baby, Nona. A baby, dear. People have been known to swell a bit when they're having babies.

Nona You've had three and you've never been that big all over. Are you sure it's not twins?

Lois (*dreading the thought*) Don't ... I can only handle one at a time. (*A packet of cigarettes in her hand*) Here, have a fag and shut up.

Nona Not for me. I've been cutting down since ... (*She fills up*) Since ... (*She gets a tissue from the bag*)

Bob (*to the audience*) Here she goes.

Lois (*without sympathy*) Now don't start—we've had a quiet day so far. (*She lights a cigarette*)

Nona (*holding back the tears*) It's all right for you, Lois. Just wait till Bill leaves you helpless. (*She sits on the stool*)

Lois Let him go. I'll never be helpless. (*She stands to inspect the "painting" on the fourth wall*) Here, that's a funny painting, isn't it? What's it supposed to be?

Nona (*busy tidying the room*) I think it's a couple. Doing it.

Lois (*looking at the "picture" from all angles*) Doing it? Doing what?

Nona Oh, Lois—you know!

Lois (*fascinated*) Hey, they're not! Are they? Oh, yeah.

Nona It's one of Bob's—you know what he's like.

Bob (*to the audience*) Oh yes, I told you I paint. Well, occasionally—on and off. The artistic side again, see.

Lois (*with sudden realization*) Hey, Nona—it's two fellas! See. They've both got little do-dahs!

Nona (*joining Lois*) I got a lemon cream sponge and I bet Jeff won't touch it. It's all yogurt with him.

Lois (*only to get Nona going*) Well, I'm very shocked by that painting and I'm going to say something. Mother won't like it.

Nona She's seen it—now come on, let's get this lot in the kitchen. (*She collects the shopping bags*) Did you get a lettuce?

Lois I got two while I was at it—and a loaf.

Nona (*going to the kitchen*) Another! Why didn't you say, Lois! I got two.

Lois (*taking her shopping bags and following Nona*) Oh well, we'll be able to feed the five thousand. Where's Mum?

Nona Chatting up the taxi driver. Come on, Mum!

Nona and Lois exit to the kitchen

Bob (*to the audience*) See what I mean? About women? I've been smothered by them ever since I was born. The only son, see. And no dad. He died— quite unexpectedly—on a Wednesday just after *This is Your Life*. They got him to hospital but——

Vera storms on. Her clothes, whilst smart, are an odd assortment of the wrong colours. She wears a hat at all times. She puts her bags on the sofa table

Vera (*shouting off to the kitchen*) If your dad was alive this'd kill him!

Bob (*to the audience*) They all say that, don't they?

Lois comes back and sits in the armchair

Vera I don't know what I've done to deserve a family like this—I don't. You've never gone short: you went to St Hilda's—special uniforms an' everything—and what for? Look at you: my Robert, well into his prime and still not married; Nona, her marriage in tatters—and you!

Lois Now don't start on me, Mother. Bill and me are perfectly happy, thank you.

Vera I should hope so—judging by your condition. How many's this?

Lois You know very well how many, Mother. It's only the fourth.

Vera You're too old to be having babies, Lois. I can't think what Bill's doing. It's all right for him: football this and football that—cricket this and cricket the other. If he was my husband I'd insist he stayed at home more often. Your father, bless him, he used to wash up for me, Hoover round, do the nappies, hang them on the line.

Bob (*imitating her*) "Still, he was a man in a million."

Vera (*unaware of Bob*) Still, he was a man in a million. (*She sniffs*) I can smell that cat. I've said it before, they should never keep a cat—not in a beautiful house like this. (*She produces a can of air-spray and proceeds to spray the room*)

Lois (*ducking to avoid the spray*) Be careful, Mother—it can kill you, can that stuff.

Vera D'you know what he charged me for this? Ninety-five. Ninety-five! Daylight robbery. Still, they're darkies—open all hours. (*She gets a shooting pain in her back*) Oh, I've got that pain again—in my back, Lois. It creases me.

Bob (*to the audience*) Ever since I can remember, Mum's had a pain in her back—but will she see a doctor?

Lois (*helping Vera to the sofa*) Have you been to the doctor?

Vera Doctor. I daren't. I dread to think what's wrong with me, Lois. They'd whip me in that hospital like ninepence. Look at your dad, bless him: "Vera," he said, "I won't be leaving this place alive." (*Without a pause*) Is this cardigan all crumpled at the back? (*She goes to the mirror*)

Lois (*smoking*) Looks all right to me.

Vera Well, you'd have to say that—you'd have me walking round like a bundle of rags.

Lois (*to herself*) You can't win.

Bob (*to the audience*) You can't win with my mum.

Vera What time's Bill picking them up from the airport?

Lois About three, I think—but they're bound to be late, you know what planes are like. (*She sits in the armchair*)

Vera I wouldn't go up in one. I like my feet firmly on the ground. (*Sitting on the sofa*) Did I tell you I was nearly run over outside Tesco's a week last Tuesday?

Lois (*with no interest*) You weren't.

Vera Without a word of a lie, Lois—I came down Albatross Street, crossed over by the library, up Chipping Alley and this fool came round the corner—must have been doing ninety—and if some woman hadn't grabbed my arm I'd have been a gonner now. I know I wouldn't have been missed, but somebody should write. (*Lowering her voice, and about Nona*) Where's she? She's had a face like a robber's dog all week.

Lois She's in the kitchen—washing lettuce and shelling peas.

Vera (*rising*) What's she shelling peas for?

Lois Leave her—you know what she is. She says Arthur loved peas with a salad.

Vera (*at the sofa table*) Don't mention Arthur to me. I'd crucify him, Lois. I would. Bugger! (*Producing a cooked chicken wrapped in foil from her shopping bag*) I got a capon, see, you can't beat home-cooking. How is she?

Lois She's all right—just leave her alone. And don't mention Arthur.

Bob (*to the audience*) Told you, didn't I—never mention Arthur.

Vera (*on her way out, carrying the chicken*) I'd best see what she's up to in there, she's never been able to cook has our Nona.

Lois (*following her to the kitchen*) Now don't start on her, Mother, she's a bag of nerves as it is.

Vera and Lois exit to the kitchen

Bob (*to the audience, crossing to* C) See what I mean? That's my mum. Vera Swift. Now, you might just be wondering what they're doing here ... Well, Jeff and me, we're on holiday in Malta—which is where it all started to go wrong, but I'll tell you all about that later. Actually, we're just on our way home and Bill's picking us up at the airport.

The telephone starts to ring

Just ignore it—the answer machine's on anyway.

Bob exits

The telephone only rings a couple of times and is answered by the machine

Bob's voice (*from the machine*) "Hello, Shotter and Swift. Sorry we're not here to take your call. Leave your number and we'll ring as soon as we can. Thanks." (*There is a bleep from the machine*)

Bill's voice (*from the machine*) "Lois! Are you there? Deaf cow! It's Bill, I'm just ringing to say the plane's in early—we'll be home sooner than I thought." (*The phone is put down at the other end*)

The Lights alter slightly

Jeff, changed after his shower and eating a raw carrot, enters from the kitchen. He carries some invoices. Bob, wearing a striped apron for cooking, enters from the kitchen. He carries a mixing bowl and wooden spoon. Perhaps it should be emphasized here that Bob and Jeff are a perfectly ordinary, happy couple

Bob Why are you eating?

Jeff (*sitting in the armchair*) You said half an hour—I can't wait that long.

Bob You amuse me.

Jeff Do I? I'm glad. (*Pause*) Why?

Bob You spend half the time eating and the other half jogging it off.
Jeff (*still reading the invoices*) Well?
Bob I think it's funny that's all.
Jeff Well, that's good. At least I eat wholesome food, not hamburgers and chips all day. Why don't you ever put on any weight?
Bob I build kitchens all day long, remember?
Jeff Talking of which, do you realize the Barrington-Smiths still owe us five hundred plus VAT?
Bob Never.
Jeff And the Scottish couple up by the golf-links—two-fifty plus VAT ... and Colin Wrigley, a supposed friend of yours, he hasn't paid at all yet.
Bob He will. Honest as the day is long old Colin.
Jeff Never do work for friends you once told me.
Bob I meant your friends ...
Jeff I sometimes think we build kitchens for sod all.
Bob You're the business brains. I'm the artistic one remember.
Jeff (*rising, not having looked at Bob*) What're we doing tonight?
Bob Taking Mum to see Auntie Trish.
Jeff (*unimpressed*) Jesus, whoopee!

Jeff exits to the kitchen still eating

Bob (*moving downstage; to the audience*) He likes it really—he does. He loves my family because he doesn't have one of his own, see. His mum's dead and he never knew his father. Actually, to tell the truth, and I know he won't mind me telling you because it doesn't seem to bother him, his mother never married, see. That's why he's called Shotter—after his mum. But he's fine—honest. In fact, as you can see, he and I are perfectly happy ... except for ... well, more about that later.

Nona rushes in, upset and followed closely by Lois

The Lights return to the previous level

Nona (*upset*) I do wish she wouldn't interfere.
Lois (*now the peacemaker*) Leave her, Nona, you know what she's like.
Bob (*winking at the audience*) Here we go again. I'll leave you to get on with it—see you later.

Bob exits DL

Nona (*sitting in an armchair blowing her nose*) Anybody would think I'd never made a salad before.
Lois She means well, Nona. It's for her precious little son, remember.
Nona (*jumping up again*) I think I'll Hoover round a bit.
Lois (*pushing her back into the armchair*) Oh, sit down and shut it. Take it easy. We're his sisters not the bloody cleaners. (*Sitting*) You've got to buck your ideas up, Nona—you're letting yourself go. Look at you—I've never seen you looking so dowdy.
Nona I don't care anymore. I've nobody to look glamorous for. (*She blows her nose again*)

Lois Oh, come off it, kid. You could still get a man. Look at sexy Cyril at the butchers. He thinks you're smashing.

Nona He's got a nervous twitch, Lois.

Lois Who's looking at his twitch, Nona? Have you seen the size of his hands? He fancies you something rotten.

Nona It's no good trying to cheer me up, Lois. I refuse to be cheered up.

Lois Oh, well, please yourself. (*Beat*) Have you started divorce proceedings yet?

Nona He's only been gone a fortnight—now will you please leave it!

Lois All right, no need to snap my head off. (*She lights a cigarette*) You know, I do like it here. Better than Albert Street, what? (*She rises and walks about looking at the room*) Where's the telly?

Nona They keep it in the den.

Lois What's the den when it's at home?

Nona It's their room for sitting in. They also use it as an office. Behind the kitchen dinette.

Silence. Lois smokes, Nona fidgets

(*Going to the windows*) I'm sure them curtains could do with a washing.

Lois Look, will you give over. You've gone cleaning mad. We were asked to get a bit of shopping and a meal, not beautify the bloody place. (*Pause*) Have they redecorated everywhere? Upstairs as well?

Nona Yes.

Lois What's their bedroom like?

Nona It's very nice. And don't go saying "their" bedroom in front of mother. She thinks Jeff has his own room. (*She sits in the armchair*)

Bob comes rushing in DL

Bob (*to the audience*) My God, I nearly forgot. Mum doesn't understand about Jeff and me, so don't be saying anything. I mean, she knows he lives here but she doesn't understand about the other, so we have to pretend. You see, more bloody lies!

Bob exits DL. *Vera enters, wearing Bob's apron but still in her hat and carrying some apples*

Vera You know, that new patio looks a proper picture in the sunshine. (*She goes to the table, puts the apples in the bowl*)

Nona Jeff did that.

Vera And I see Robert's had a new back gate fitted.

Nona Jeff did that too.

Vera (*annoyed*) Look, Nona, not everything's Jeff you know. My Robert does his share around this house.

Nona I didn't say he didn't, did I?

Vera No, but you inferred it. And there's no need for snappiness. Just because I washed the lettuce.

Lois Oh, stop it, both of you. Does it matter who washes the soddin' lettuce.

Vera There's no particular need for her to snap at me, Lois.

Lois I told you to leave her, Mother. You know she's a lot on her mind.

Vera A lot on her mind—don't you think I've a lot on my mind? What with you lot. I lie awake in that bed and worry myself stupid.

Lois There's no need. We're fine.

Vera Fine, Lois. Fine? Every time I look round you're expecting again.

Lois Mother, there's at least three years between each of my boys. You talk as if I'm dropping 'em every five minutes!

Vera I wish I hadn't come today. There's always trouble when I try to lend a helping hand.

Lois Oh, don't start all that now.

Vera Well, it's true. Sometimes I think I'd be better off in a home, then you wouldn't have to bother about me at all. (*She sits on the stool*)

Lois I know, then we could leave you there to rot.

Vera (*narrowing her eyes at Lois*) You've got a very nasty streak to your nature, Lois. And it doesn't come from me! Or your dad, bless him.

Lois (*looking about*) There's not a sign of a bloody ashtray anywhere.

Vera And you smoke too much. That baby will come out covered in soot!

Lois (*rising, leaving the room*) I'll get a saucer or something.

Lois exits to the kitchen

Vera She's changed just lately, has Lois. I think she should see somebody. (*Over sympathetic*) Are you all right, pet? (*She joins Nona*)

Nona (*blowing her nose*) I'm fine as long as I don't think about anything.

Vera You should get away, love—a world cruise—do you good.

Nona What on, Mother—milk bottle tops?

Vera I'll pay. What are mothers for? I've always got a bit put by. In fact, the way I'm feeling I might just come with you.

Nona (*dreading the thought*) No, thanks—I'd sooner stop at home.

Lois returns from the kitchen with a saucer for an ashtray

Vera I'm just saying, Lois, Nona should treat herself.

Lois Yes, to sexy Cyril at the butchers.

Vera Don't talk smutty, Lois. It's all right for you, you've got the life of Old Riley. Just wait till you're manless like me and Nona here, that'll wipe the smile off your face.

Lois Thank you, Mother. (*Stirring it*) Have you seen that painting?

Vera (*admiring the "painting"*) Isn't it beautiful? You've got a very talented brother, you two, and I don't think you appreciate him. Look at the way the light falls—and those flesh tones. It'd win a prize.

Lois (*winking at Nona*) What's it supposed to be?

Vera Trust you. You wouldn't know one painting from another. It's quite obvious what it is—it's two brothers having a dance.

Silence. Vera produces knitting from her bag and sits on the sofa

By the way, I'll not be coming over to your house tomorrow, Lois, if you don't mind.

Lois Oh, Mum—I thought you were coming to Sunday tea as usual?

Vera Well, I won't if you don't mind. I'd rather stop at home. (*To herself*) I know where I'm not wanted.

Lois (*raising her eyes to heaven*) What're you on about now?

Vera (*preparing her knitting*) I'm not made of stone, Lois. The last time I came to your house, Bill was very insulting.

Lois Insulting? Bill? He never said a word.

Vera That's what I mean. I may as well not have been there. I find it very hurtful, Lois. I dread to think what your dad would have said.

Lois Oh, well, please yourself. The kids will miss you anyway.

Vera (*casting on*) Well, at least somebody will. And there's another thing——

Nona (*to herself*) I feel very bilious.

Vera I think I'll have a change at Christmas, too.

Lois Christmas!

Vera Yes, Christmas. I feel it's time for a change.

Lois Mother, it's only July. We might all be dead and buried by then!

Vera (*taking offence as usual*) That's nice—very nice! (*Rounding on Nona*) Did you hear that, Nona?

Nona (*preoccupied*) Sorry?

Lois You know what I mean, Mother. It's a bit early to be discussing Christmas, surely.

Vera I like to know where I am, Lois. I like to plan ahead. When you get to my time of life and you're all alone in the world, you like to think you'll be amongst your loved ones at a time like Christmas.

Lois looks to heaven but remains silent

Bill's mother doesn't like me. All right, I know what you're going to say——

Lois I wasn't going to say anything.

Vera (*turning nasty*) No, Lois, because there's no need. You saw how Bill's mother——

Lois Doris, Mother—I wish you'd call her Doris and not Bill's mother all the time.

Vera I don't like her, I never did like her, and if you knew what I knew about her brother . . . well, the least said!

Nona (*never having heard this*) What?

Lois All that died with the ark . . . there's only you who remembers.

Vera Yes, well, at least we don't have anybody funny in our family. And I won't forget that turkey leg in a hurry. She knows what my stomach's like, but oh no: breast for her, breast for Bill and the kids, but you and me, what did we get? Legs! (*To Nona*) It was very hurtful, Nona.

Nona (*trying to stay out of it*) Yes, I'm sure it was. (*As if it might help*) Arthur and I had pork. (*She is upset by the memory of happier times*)

Vera (*knitting furiously*) No, I've given it a lot of thought and I think it's time for a change.

Lois You can't come here. Bob and Jeff go abroad for Christmas.

Vera Who said anything about coming here? No, my mind's made up, I shall spend this Christmas with Nona.

Nona (*ashen with dread*) Me?

Vera Yes, pet. You'll be on your own, and you won't have much money coming in now that selfish swine has left you high and dry.

Lois That's right, Mother, cheer her up.

Vera Well, the poor bitch will be on her own, won't she?

Lois It's six months away yet, he might have come back by then.

Nona (*hopefully*) Yes, he might.

Vera He won't be back, mark my words.

Silence. Nona is depressed, Lois is furious

Did I tell you I saw him?

Nona (*ever more hopeful*) Arthur? Where? (*She joins Vera on the sofa*)

Vera Don't ask. It'll only upset you. (*Addressing Lois as if Nona wasn't there*) He was at the fifty-nine bus stop with her—Brenda Brierley from Boots. Kissing and cuddling. I'll tell you what, Lois, I didn't know where to put my face, and you know me—I'm not easily shocked!

Nona (*rushing from the room*) I think I'm going to be sick.

Nona exits to the kitchen. Bob enters DL, *watching Nona rush out*

Vera (*unaware of Bob*) That girl's heading for a nervous breakdown, Lois— mark my words.

Bob (*to the audience*) See what I mean? Happy families is this. Life's rich pattern is unfolding before your very eyes. How're you getting on?

Vera (*to Lois*) D'you think she's upset again?

Lois (*with only a hint of sarcasm*) I should think she just might be, Mother. Why can't you just keep your mouth shut?

Vera I'm that girl's mother, Lois. If I can't be honest, who can?

Lois I'd best see to her.

Lois exits to the kitchen

Bob (*to the audience*) Lois spends all her time keeping the peace. She has done since she was two ...

Vera (*still knitting, to Bob*) And why aren't you married?

Bob (*to the audience*) Here we go. Once a fortnight, regular as clockwork, whenever she gets me on my own, she asks me that. (*He takes a magazine from the table and joins Vera*)

Vera You'll have people thinking you're not right. I was married and had a child by the time I was eighteen.

Bob I'm all right, Mother, don't be going on about it. (*He sits with Vera*)

Vera You're not all right, Robert. A nice boy like you.

Bob I am not a nice boy, Mum.

Vera (*not listening*) Why haven't you got a girl-friend? Some smart young woman—well set up, thinks a lot of herself? Look at Sylvia Twine, what a lovely girl, you liked her.

Bob I was only seven, Mother, and she was six. The years have rolled by since then.

Vera Well, it's the future I worry about. I won't be here for ever, you know—who'll worry about you then?

Bob (*reading the magazine*) I don't need anyone to worry about me. I can worry about meself.

Vera (*standing, adjusting her cardigan*) D'you think this cardigan's too big? (*She goes to look in the mirror*)

Bob It looks fine.

Vera I'm not so sure. I like my garments to fit snugly round my bust. You know your Auntie Trish is very ill.

Bob (*preoccupied*) Is she?

Vera It's a miracle she's still with us. He led her a dog's life you know. I think I've told you. (*She sits in the armchair*)

Bob (*with no interest*) Yes—constantly.

Vera Sex on demand whenever he felt like it. It's no way to live. He was very . . . well, very . . . you know!

Bob Had a huge sex-drive, did he? Uncle Cedric.

Vera He had a huge something or other—but I don't care to think about it. She had seventeen stitches you know.

Bob (*confused*) Who?

Vera My sister. Trish. When she fell downstairs.

Bob (*lost*) Oh.

Vera (*standing*) You're not listening, Robert, are you? You're like our Nona and Lois. I sometimes think I'd be better off out of it. I do. And you shouldn't keep a cat in a house like this!

Vera storms off to the kitchen

Bob (*to the audience, lowering his magazine*) You can see what she's like, can't you? She moves entirely in a world of her own. Of course, it's not her fault—we are what we are, aren't we? How could I tell her about Jeff and me? A while ago, Lois said she must know . . .

The Lights change

Lois enters from the kitchen

Lois (*to Bob*) She must know, Bob. You've been together as long as Bill and me. Surely she must realize what's going on. (*She sits on the sofa with Bob*)

Bob Why should she? It's out of her experience.

Lois I suppose so.

Bob She's a little woman, with a little mind, moving in her own little world. She never goes anywhere, never sees anybody—apart from us and Auntie Trish. She knows nothing.

Lois Nor do we. And I'd hardly call you and Jeff gadabouts. You're as dreary and respectable as we are. As Nona and Arthur, for heaven's sake.

Bob Their marriage is nearly over.

Lois Cobblers! Do you believe that? He'll be back. As soon as Brenda gets fed up washing his socks and underpants and discovers his dirty magazines under the bed.

Bob (*agog*) No. Really?

Lois Oh, you don't know the half. Why haven't they had any kids—tell me that. Because, when it comes to the crunch, he can't even get it up let alone keep it up!

Bob I was always led to believe that all was well.

Lois Lies, love, all lies.

Bob When did she tell you all this?

Lois Oh, about a fortnight after they were married. (*Lowering her voice*) Apparently, on their wedding night——

Bob (*covering his ears*) Don't! I don't want to hear anymore!

Lois There you are then. And I'll tell you another thing—it suits our Nona down to the ground. She doesn't like all the other. She likes to make out she does, but I know different. She's quite content with a pot of tea, her feet up and the telly.

Bob Then why can't they just admit it to each other?

Lois You know, for a pervert you're very naïve.

Lois exits to the kitchen

Bob (*to the audience*) Am I?

Slight lighting change and back to the slow, easy pace between Bob and Jeff as they are now. Bob reads his magazine again

Jeff enters from the patio, eating an apple

(*At length, to Jeff*) Would you say I was naïve?

Jeff Naïve? Why?

Bob No, be honest. Would you?

Jeff To be honest, yes, I think you are naïve. Just a bit. Why do you ask?

Bob I'm just reading here . . . there's this chap, he couldn't make love to his wife unless she was wrapped up in brown paper and tied with string.

Jeff (*thinking about it*) Like screwing a parcel.

Bob Aren't you shocked?

Jeff No. People do funny things.

Bob We don't. We're quite normal compared to that.

Jeff We are normal.

Bob Are we?

Jeff Normal and naïve. What's for supper?

Bob (*back to his magazine*) Fish.

Jeff Not fried I hope.

Bob Fried for me with lashings of chips, steamed for you—with gunge.

Jeff (*turning to go*) Good.

Bob Jeff?

Jeff Bob?

Bob Are you happy?

Jeff I'd tell you if I wasn't. Wouldn't I?

Bob You did before, remember?

Jeff I do.

Bob And you're over that?

Jeff (*not really an answer*) You worry too much.

Jeff exits to the kitchen

Bob (*to the audience*) I suppose you're wondering what all that was about. Well, you see, that's why we went to Malta—to try and straighten things out. We went through a bad patch and ...

The Lights return to the previous level

Lois enters from the kitchen, followed by Vera

Hang on, they're back—I'll talk to you later, when I get back from Malta.

Bob exits

Vera The last thing I wanted was to upset you.

Lois Look, Mother, could we just forget Christmas. There might be a nuclear war before then! (*She is near the patio doors*)

Vera (*sitting on the sofa, back to her knitting*) You've got a very peculiar side to your nature, Lois, and it hasn't always been there. I suppose you get it from Doris—as you seem to spend more time with her than you do with your own mother.

Lois I spend no more time with Doris than I do with you, so don't start all that.

Vera I suppose she's over at your house now. Looking after the kids. I notice I never get asked.

Lois Only because they give you a headache.

Vera (*not listening, knitting*) Anybody would think they only had one granny. Do you like this blouse? I got it in C and A's.

Lois Very nice.

Vera They had it in magenta and moss green but I thought this was very elegant. What d'you think?

Lois I've told you—I like the blouse.

Nona enters from the kitchen

Nona (*ever worried, to Vera*) I hope you didn't put butter on the bread. Jeff likes that stuff in a tub in the fridge.

Vera Why does everything have to revolve round Jeff in this house? Our Robert was fetched up with butter. If you ask me, I think Jeff is taking liberties with our Robert.

Lois (*to herself*) It's one way of putting it, I suppose.

Vera (*not catching the remark*) Did you speak, Lois?

Nona You know, I'm sure I should run the Hoover over—just to be on the safe side.

Lois Look, Nona, just sit down, you're making me giddy, jumping about.

Nona sits in the armchair biting her nails, Vera knits, Lois smokes

Vera Where is Malta anyway?

Lois Italy—Africa—that way on. Nona?

Nona Don't ask me. I can get lost finding my way home.

Vera (*knitting*) I only hope to God Robert hasn't been mixing with them foreign women. Go to bed with anybody I'm told.

Lois Who? Our Robert?

Vera (*with a cold stare*) The trouble with you, our Lois, you try to be clever and it doesn't always do to be clever.

Lois All I'm saying is I'm sure you don't have to worry about our Robert mixing with women.

Vera (*offended*) And why not? You talk as if there's something the matter with him.

Lois (*sorry she got into this*) There's nothing the matter with him, but he's with Jeff, isn't he, Jeff'll look after him.

Vera He's old enough to look after himself, thank you. (*Knitting furiously*) I don't see why they have to go off on holiday together anyway—it's unnatural.

Lois What's unnatural about it? They're friends, aren't they—you don't go on holiday with people you hate. They get on well.

Vera How do you know? They might be rowing every five minutes for all you know.

Lois Oh, come off it, Mother, now you're just being awkward. Have you ever seen Bob and Jeff rowing, be honest, have you?

Vera (*nearly lost for words but, as usual, finding an answer*) Only because our Robert's not the rowing type. He's like me—he'd run a mile from a row. Now look what you've made me do—I've dropped a stitch!

Lois (*happy to change the subject*) What're you knitting now? I thought you bought all your clothes.

Vera (*pointing at Lois's stomach*) I'm knitting for that, aren't I? If it was left to you the poor little mite would have nothing to wear.

Lois (*genuinely touched*) Thanks, Mum. You've got a heart of gold really, haven't you? (*She joins Vera on the sofa*)

Vera Don't try and soft soap me. I won't be soft-soaped. But if the day ever dawns when I can't put myself out to knit a little matinee jacket for my granddaughter . . .

Lois Oh, it's going to be a girl, is it?

Vera About time it was. If only to stop that husband of yours thinking you can produce a football team.

A long silence. Vera sings to herself

Nona I think I've got a migraine coming on.

No-one replies. Nona looks at her watch, Vera knits, Lois looks through a magazine

Vera Did I tell you Jessie Cosgrove dropped dead in Fitton's?

Pause

One minute buying a quarter of boiled ham—the next, dead on the floor.

Pause

You never know, do you?

No-one replies

I'll be surprised if I'm still here at Christmas.

The peace and quiet is about to be shattered. A car pulls up outside

Lois A car. It can't be them, surely?
Nona (*jumping up*) They're early. I said I should have got that kettle on, didn't I? Now I'm all behind ... (*She is about to exit to the kitchen*)
Vera Keep calm, Nona. They won't want a fuss. Let them get in, put their feet up, unwind a bit.
Nona They're bound to want a decent cup of tea, Mother, you know what the water's like abroad.
Vera (*rising*) Stop mithering—stay and welcome your brother home.
Lois (*rising*) You'd think they'd been to Mars and back.
Vera Lois! Just shut it!

All three women stand waiting to welcome the homecomers

Bob enters from the street door, now dressed in holiday clothes, an "Air Malta" bag over his shoulder and carrying an artist's folding easel

(*With open arms, all smiles*) My son, my son. Did you bring me a present?
Bob (*ignoring her, going straight upstairs*) Some fucking holiday that was!

Bob exits upstairs

Vera (*shocked*) What did he say? Did he swear?
Lois No, Mother, that's Maltese I expect.
Nona He seems a bit upset, doesn't he?
Lois You could say that, Nona.
Vera (*shouting up the stairs*) Robert, pet, what is it?
Lois Oh, leave him.
Vera I'll bet he's lost his luggage—you read about it, don't you?

Jeff enters from the street in a hurry, now dressed in holiday clothes

Jeff (*breathless*) He's a moody sod—where did he go?

Nona points upstairs

Lois What the hell's going on, Jeff?
Jeff (*going upstairs*) Tell you later—we had a bit of an upset.

Jeff exits upstairs

Vera (*shouting after him*) I suppose this is all your fault. (*To Lois, self-satisfied*) Never row did you say—what's this?

Bill enters carrying suitcases. A quiet, unassuming man

Bill Where shall I put these?
Lois What's going on, Bill?
Bill How should I know? Nobody tells me anything. Where d'you want these?
Lois Leave them out there, don't clutter this room up.

Bill deposits the cases out of sight in the hall

Bob and Jeff can be heard rowing loudly upstairs

Bob (*off*) Look, Jeff, just piss off will you!

Jeff (*off*) Not until you tell me what all this performance is about!

Bob (*off*) You know bloody well what it's all about. Now stop following me about, will you!

Jeff (*off*) If you'd just allow me to explain——

Bob (*off, overlapping*) I'm warning you, you come one step nearer and I'll smash your stupid face in! Now get lost—twat!

Vera (*over the above*) Listen to it, we'll have the neighbours thinking we're gypsies.

Lois (*quietly enjoying all the fuss*) Oh, well, I'm having a fag. (*She lights a cigarette and goes to the windows*)

Nona (*on edge*) My gateau will never be defrosted in time now.

Bill returns

Why are you so early, Bill?

Bill I rang to tell you but nobody heard me. Is that kettle on? (*He takes his jacket off, hangs it on the dining-chair, takes the newspaper from the pocket and sits in the armchair* R)

There is more noise from upstairs: banging doors, etc.

Bob (*off, shouting*) Bollocks! Now sod off!

Vera That's it—I'm not putting up with all this. (*She shouts upstairs*) Here! Pack it in, will you!

The shouting stops. Silence

(*Coming into the room*) Is all this your fault, Bill?

Bill Look, Vera, don't start on me. I was told to pick 'em up at the airport, so I picked 'em up at the airport—right? Right!

Jeff (*off*) How many more times have I to tell you—it was all perfectly innocent, Bob!

Bob comes rushing downstairs, harassed

Bob (*shouting back to Jeff*) Oh, bollocks, Jeff! Don't give me all that crap! (*On his way out to the garden, to the others*) If he comes anywhere near me, I'm warning you, I'm going to land him one!

Bob exits into the garden. Jeff comes hurrying down the stairs after Bob

Jeff (*calling after Bob*) I don't know why you're making all this fuss over nothing anyway.

Nona Did you have a nice holiday, Jeff?

Jeff (*going into the garden*) I thought so, Nona. (*Calling out to Bob*) I've told you umpteen times—nothing happened on Gozo!

Jeff exits into the garden

Vera
Nona } (*together*) Gozo?
Lois

Vera (*sitting, exhausted*) All this is making me ill. I can't live like this, not at my time of life.

Lois (*untroubled*) Well, it makes a change, I suppose. Were they like this in the car, Bill?

Bill Not a word. Jeff sat next to me and Bob in the back. I could tell they had the hump—I thought it best to keep out of it. What's for tea?

Vera (*sharply*) Chicken salad—breast!

Bill (*to Lois*) What's up with her?

Lois Oh, leave it. (*Holding her stomach*) This baby's playing up here.

Vera I'm not surprised. You'll have a miscarriage at this rate.

Nona I'm going to the kitchen—I'm all on edge.

Lois I'll come with you, no use standing here like a lemon.

Lois and Nona exit to the kitchen

Vera That baby'll be born demented the way she keeps jumping up and down.

No reply. Bill is reading the sports page

Did you hear what I said?

Nothing

Oh, I see. It's ignore Vera time, is it? (*She gets up and goes to the window*) I suppose you couldn't care less that my son is having a nervous break-down.

Bill (*reading*) I've learned to keep my mouth shut, Vera.

Vera (*seeing something dreadful in the garden*) My God—our Robert's going to kill him!

Vera rushes out into the garden

Bill watches her go and raises his eyes to heaven

Bill (*to himself*) It's like a bloody madhouse this. (*He goes back to his paper*)

The Lights dim slightly leaving the area around Bill's chair more brightly lit

Bob enters from his area DL. *He leans against the proscenium*

Bob (*to the audience, smiling*) It's all right, I'm quite safe. Were you worried about me? You see what I mean though—into the most ordered lives a little chaos must fall. You must be wondering what all that's about. All that mention of Gozo. Don't talk to me about Gozo—I hate the bloody place and I've never even been! (*He smiles down at Bill*) What about Bill, eh? I said you'd like him. A picture of domestic tranquillity, isn't he? Never complains, seldom raises his voice. You wouldn't believe it but he was partly to blame for all the trouble. I didn't find this out till later, but he and Jeff had a conversation, it seems, sometime back ...

Jeff enters from upstairs

The lighting evens out but not to full yet, to indicate the past

Jeff Bill?

Bob exits DL

Bill (*folding his paper*) Jeff?

Jeff Can I ask you something? (*He stands near Bill*)

Bill As long as you're not after money.

Jeff What do you think of Bob and me?

Bill How d'you mean, what do I think?

Jeff Well, I mean—do we worry you at all?

Bill (*genuinely puzzled*) Worry me? Why should you worry me?

Jeff No, well . . . I've often wondered if we do.

Bill (*the penny drops*) Oh, I see—you mean . . . ! Good God, no. Why? Does it worry you?

Jeff What?

Bill Being back to front or whatever you say. I won't call it gay because I've got an uncle who's a bit of a teapot but he's the most miserable bugger I've ever come across.

Jeff He's like us, is he?

Bill Not a bit. He goes on marches an' stuff like that—poncing through Manchester carrying a banner, letting everybody know his business, wearing a T-shirt with "Gay Pride" written all over it. Then he gets annoyed when nobody's interested. I mean, I'm a Catholic but it's not the sort of thing you go telling everybody, is it? (*He laughs*) You and Bob don't go marching, do you?

Jeff We've never felt the need, I suppose.

Bill No, well, you've got each other, haven't you? My uncle's a bit of a loner, I doubt if he's got any friends at all. (*Pause*) What's on your mind then?

Jeff Oh, I don't know . . . do you ever get the feeling you're stuck in a rut? (*He sits on the sofa arm*)

Bill All the time. It happens to all of us, lad. That feeling of knowing you're stuck with the same person for ever—the same job, day in, day out.

Jeff That's it.

Bill It's called married life.

Jeff Yeah. It's no different with me and Bob than it is with you and Lois.

Bill I never thought it was. Except for the kids of course. At least I have them—and another one on the way. And since they're all boys I can play football with 'em, take them to cricket. I love all that, you see.

Jeff You get bored with it all though? The routine, the lack of excitement, the sheer bloody ordinariness of it all?

Bill Course I do. But if I get sick of her, God forgive me, I can go down for a pint, can't I? Make eyes at the barmaid, pass a comment about her tits, you know the sort of thing. Pretend to be a real man. But there's nothing like coming home to her. She always makes me laugh. She's very funny is our Lois. And lovable. Don't you find?

Jeff Oh, yes, I do. And I like Nona. She's funny in a totally different way. Then there's Vera.

Bill (*his smile fading*) She's just bloody funny full stop. I could put my hands round her throat sometimes—but she's harmless. (*Pause*) You know what I think's wrong with you and Bob? Lois thinks it too—we often talk about you both.

Jeff No. What?

Bill Tell me to mind my own business if you want—but you're never apart.

Jeff I know.

Bill I mean, you work together, eat together, live together—sleep together. It's a lot, mate. At least I'm out of the house eight/nine hours a day. No wonder you get pissed off with it all.

Jeff But Bob loves it all, you see?

Bill Does he? How d'you know?

Jeff Well, he just does—I know he does.

Bill Have you asked him?

Jeff Well . . . no . . . not really.

Bill There you are then. How d'you know he's not as bored as you. You should get away, both of you—find a quiet spot, go on holiday. Talk things over.

Jeff Do you reckon?

Bill When a couple stop communicating, mate, it's a bad sign. If there's anything wrong in our house, Lois is the first to sort it out. (*Pause, he finds the next thing rather difficult to say*) Have you never . . . I mean, have you never . . .

Jeff What?

Bill You know what I mean . . . have you never had a bit on the side like . . . another bloke?

Jeff Well, actually . . . no, I haven't. Not since I met Bob.

Bill (*amazed*) You haven't!

Jeff No. Why, have you been unfaithful?

Bill (*after thinking about it*) Actually—no, I haven't. Mind you, I'd never tell anybody—I mean, the chaps at work—I'd never be able to hold my head up. Course, it's all right these days, you can blame having to be faithful on HIV, can't you?

Jeff smiles but doesn't answer: he's thoughtful

Course, you know what our trouble is, don't you?

Jeff What?

Bill We're behind the times, mate. Dead old fashioned. We're a dying breed, we are.

The two men are silent, reflective

Tell me, I hope you don't think I'm prying, but don't you ever fancy a bit of straight?

Jeff Straight?

Bill (*with a wicked grin*) You know. Crumpet. Birds. The ladies.

Jeff I did use to.

Bill (*intrigued*) Get away. What went wrong?

Jeff (*standing*) It's too long a story. I might tell you someday. (*Pause, then quietly*) I'd love kids, you see, Bill.

Bill Yes, I bet you would. I can just see it. You'd make good dads, you an' old Bob. But you're in dead shtook, see, because children have to have mums. Like Vera. Like Doris. Like our Lois. (*Pause*) You should have a word with Bob, you know, I'm sure he'd understand.

Jeff (*laughing*) I don't think so somehow.

Bill You know, it's a pity old Vera doesn't know about you two. She'd sort you out in no time.

Jeff Give over.

Bill Wanna bet? She's a wily old bird is our Vera. Oh, I know she's a flaming nuisance most of the time, but you mark my words, I bet she'd turn up trumps. Pity you can't tell her, isn't it?

Jeff I'd tell her tomorrow. It's Bob. He thinks she'd have a stroke.

Bill She probably would, poor cow. Who's to say. (*Unfolding his paper again*) Sorry I can't be more helpful, Jeff.

Jeff (*more at ease now*) Actually, you have been. It's always good to talk. Thanks.

Bill You're welcome, mate. (*He stops. He thinks*) Here, can I ask you something?

Jeff What?

Bill This might sound a bit ... (*Bashful*) Ah, no, I couldn't.

Jeff (*laughing*) Go on, say it.

Bill Well ... No, I couldn't.

Jeff Get on with it, for Christ's sake!

Bill (*it is a very difficult question*) Well, I've often wondered ... (*He can't ask*)

Jeff Oh, I see ... you mean ... me and Bob, like. (*Smiling at Bill's embarrassment*) Is that it?

Bill Well—sort of.

Jeff (*teasing him*) You'll just have to find out, won't you? (*Playfully he sits on Bill's knee*)

Bill (*panic, pushing him off*) Here—leave off!

Jeff (*laughing*) You're blushing. (*On his way to the kitchen*) Can I get you a Coke? Cool you down.

Bill It's not me who needs cooling down, mate!

Suddenly all the Lights come up to full as before. It is the present

Jeff, Lois and Nona enter from the kitchen. Vera enters from the garden

Nona We're very worried about you and Bob, Jeff.

Lois Why don't you tell us what's going on ...

Jeff (*different now he's back in the present*) I can't think what all the fuss is about. Bob's gone and got the bloody hump, that's all. In fact, if you must know, he's had the hump all holiday.

Vera There must be a good reason. Our Robert doesn't get the hump for nothing. He's like his father, very sensitive.

Jeff Like his mother you mean—bloody awkward!

Vera What did he say, Lois?

Lois Oh, leave it, Mother, it's none of our business.

Vera None of our business? If my son's sitting out there in the garden with tears in his eyes I consider it very much my business.

Nona (*worried*) Is our Robert crying? (*She sits on the sofa arm*)

Vera Just keep out of it, Nona. This is a mother's business. (*To Jeff*) Now, come along, young man, what's happened? (*She sits in the* L *armchair*)

Jeff Nothing's happened, so keep your nose out, Vera.

Vera If you've been introducing my son to party girls and shady night-clubs ...

Jeff (*to Lois*) What is she on about, Lois? Vera, I do wish you wouldn't talk bollocks! (*He sits at the table*)

Vera And we've had quite enough of that, there's been far too much smutty talk around here today from the likes of you.

Jeff Oh, I'm "the likes of you" now, am I? Look, Vera——

Vera Mrs Swift, if you don't mind, seeing we've fallen out. Everything was fine till this happened. We were as happy as ninepence, weren't we, Lois?

Lois (*enjoying it all*) We were, Mother. Bill?

Bill (*reading his paper, irritated*) What?

Lois We were happy as ninepence.

Bill Sod off. You realize I'm missing a day's cricket for all this lot.

Vera (*crossing to Bill, turning on him*) Oh dear, I am sorry. Giving my son a helping hand has put you out, has it, Bill? Rather selfish I would have thought.

Bill (*amazed*) Me? Selfish? Me? (*He moves to the stool and sits*)

Lois (*stirring it*) Well, you are a bit selfish, Bill.

Bill Get lost. Pregnant pratt!

Lois Did you hear that, Mother—did you hear what he called me?

Vera Oh, go on, our Lois—poke fun—it's all you're fit for.

Nona (*almost to herself*) I feel very bilious.

Vera If your dad was alive he'd turn in his grave—seeing my being upset in my own son's house by an outsider.

Jeff Outsider now. This happens to be my house as well, Mrs Swift! (*He stands behind Vera*)

Vera (*to Lois*) I'm sorry—did he speak?

Nona I think I'm having a hot flush here ...

Vera (*to Jeff*) And who placed the deposit on this house, might I ask?

Lois Here we go.

Vera (*to Lois*) You keep out of this, young woman.

Lois Sorry, keep your mouth shut, Lois.

Jeff All right, so you put down the deposit—and Christ don't we know it— but we paid you back as soon as we got on our feet.

Bob enters quietly from the garden

Nona (*seeing Bob*) Sshhh! (*She stands*)

Vera (*not hearing this*) I'll tell you something, young man——

Nona (*much louder*) SSHHH!

Vera Please don't shush me, Nona—I refuse to be shushed.
Nona Bob's here.

Everyone is silent

Vera (*sitting on the sofa*) Hello, pet. All right, love?

Silence. Bob is calmer now, looks round at them all then goes over and sits beside Vera on the sofa

   That's right, love, sit beside your old mother.

She attempts to put an arm round him but he resists. An awkward silence

Nona (*trying to be cheerful*) Did you have a nice holiday, Bob?
Bob (*staring over at Jeff*) Not bad, thanks.
Jeff Feeling better, are you?
Bob (*moody*) I'm fine, thanks.
Jeff (*recognizing the symptoms*) I see. That means you're not. I hope you're going to apologize for creating all this fuss.
Vera I don't see why Robert has to apologize.
Lois Keep out of it, Mother. (*Calmly to Bob*) What's Malta like—nice is it, love?
Bob Like a building site—on heat. Why don't you ask him how he enjoyed Gozo!
Jeff Here we go.
Vera (*mystified*) Gozo? What's Gozo?
Bob And ask him about Terri.

All except Bob and Jeff are in the dark

Jeff Look, let's leave Terri out of it.
Bob (*as if only he and Jeff were present*) Oh, yes—we mustn't mention Terri—and we mustn't mention Gozo!
Jeff (*ditto*) You could have come with us—I enjoy sightseeing, Bob. You prefer to stay put and paint, read, sunbathe!
Lois (*tactfully*) Would you like us to leave?
Bill (*rising*) What a good idea . . .

Lois glares at him. He sits

Jeff Not at all. You're more than welcome in our house! (*He glares at Vera*)
Vera If you ask me there's more to this than meets the eye. Who is this Terri? Not a drug smuggler, I hope.
Jeff That woman's mad, she should be put away.
Vera Robert, I demand to know what's been going on. I'm your mother, mothers understand.
Bob (*still looking at Jeff*) You wouldn't understand this.
Vera Is it the business? Have you got into trouble?
Jeff (*to Bob*) If you told her what she should have known years ago——
Bob Pack that in, Jeff. She's my mother. I'll tell her only what I want to tell her.
Vera (*mystified again*) Lois—Nona, what are they talking about?

Lois (*always knowing the right thing to do*) Come on, Mother, let's get the tea ready. And you, Nona. I suspect this is personal business.
Vera I want to hear this. If there's something queer going on I want to know what it is.

Lois and Nona march Vera off to the kitchen

They have gone. Silence

Jeff (*at length*) I'm sorry about all this, Bill.
Bill Oh, don't worry about me, lads. I'm fine.
Bob We should have had a separate holiday, then you could have done what you liked.
Jeff I've been saying that for months, Bob.
Bob (*almost contradicting himself*) Oh, so you want us to be apart, then?
Jeff I don't want us to be apart for Christ's sake. We just need a flaming break, Bob! Bill, tell him.
Bill (*rising*) Look, lads, I'm going for a pee. Don't drag me into it, eh? (*At the foot of the stairs, trying to be cheerful*) Shall I have one for you as well?

Bill gets no response and exits upstairs

Silence. After a while, Jeff goes over to Bob, sits on the sofa and puts an arm around him. For a moment their closeness is quite touching: their differences could be settled now but it isn't easy for Bob yet

Bob (*getting up and moving away*) Gerroff!
Jeff What's wrong with you?
Bob (*heated*) What's wrong with me—did you say what's wrong with me?
Jeff All right, calm down, we've had quite enough histrionics from Vera.
Bob I just want to know what's going on. We go on holiday, to be together remember, because you're feeling, what was it—"bored", "stale", "in need of a change"—are those the words you used?
Jeff In need of someone to talk to, Bob.
Bob I see. You can't talk to me then?
Jeff Of course I can—and that's what I thought we'd do in Malta. Why else do you think I chose such a dead and alive hole? I thought we could sort things out.
Bob What things? If there's any sorting out to be done we can do it here— we don't have to go halfway across the world.
Jeff Oh, come off it, Bob. What chance do we get here? We're either working—or sleeping—or you're cooking or cleaning.
Bob Or you're off out, frigging jogging!
Jeff All right, so I'm as much to blame as you. I accept that. But it doesn't alter the fact that we spend most of our waking hours in silence.
Bob So, if it was your intention to put that right on holiday why did you pick up the first thing that came along and sod off every day?
Jeff Terri picked me up. And only because I was on my own. You were too busy doing bloody housework: washing underpants in the bathroom sink for Christ's sake. It was supposed to be a holiday—a break from all that crap.

Bob Look, it's you who doesn't like hotels, remember.

Jeff OK, so we prefer an apartment because we enjoy the privacy.

Bob Right, and we have to eat but you don't like cooking; we have to have clean clothes but you don't like washing. D'you think I enjoy acting like a bloody big woman? One of us has to do these things.

Jeff But we could have eaten out. Gone for walks. *Talked* for God's sake!

Bob You were never there, Jeff. Too busy chatting up Terri.

Jeff I thought you'd be happy sketching—painting—you usually are on holiday. But, oh, no, you were too busy getting the hump.

Bob (*shouting*) Are you surprised?

Jeff Keep your voice down—they'll hear.

Bob I don't care who hears, I want this out once and for all. I've just had my holiday ruined by a complete stranger.

Jeff (*becoming heated*) We would have had it out on the plane, but oh no, you insisted on us sitting ten rows apart pretending we didn't know each other. Then we get to the airport and Bill's waiting for us. Then we get home and your tribe are here. We can't even talk here without Vera getting hysterical . . . (*He gets up*)

At this point there is a dreadful commotion off

Vera and Lois drag on Nona who appears to be having some sort of choking fit

From here on, everyone talks at once and the speeches overlap

Bob My mother doesn't get hysterical . . .

Vera (*almost hysterical*) Oh, my God, quick, Robert, my beautiful Nona's having a fit . . . call somebody . . . get a doctor . . . the poor bitch is choking to death . . . !

Bob (*ignoring Vera and co.*) All I want is the truth, Jeff: what happened on Gozo . . . ?

Lois (*to Vera, handling Nona*) Calm down, Mother, calm down—she's only swallowed a piece of lettuce . . . !

Lois and Vera help Nona to the L armchair

Jeff (*to Bob*) How many more times must I tell you . . . nothing happened on Gozo . . . I wish I'd never heard of bloody Gozo . . . ! (*He sits in the R armchair*)

At this moment, Bill comes downstairs

Nona (*in a state, coughing*) I'm so embarrassed—it went down the wrong hole—I'm so sorry.

Bob (*to Jeff, louder to cover the distraction*) Oh, come off it, you expect me to believe all that? You stayed there all night and nothing happened? Balls! (*He comes over to Jeff*)

Bill (*ignoring all the fuss*) Did you know there was a half-starved cat in your lavatory? Shall I feed it . . . ?

No-one takes any notice of Bill

Jeff (*loudly to Bob*) We simply got carried away exploring the island ...
then we had a meal and before we knew it we'd missed the last ferry
back ... !

Bill Does nobody care about that poor cat?

Bob I wasn't born last week, Jeff. Come on, admit it: the pair of you had it
all planned—some nice cosy little hotel, was it?

Bill (*going to the kitchen*) Oh, well, sod the lot of you ... !

Bill exits to the kitchen

Vera (*attending to Nona, shouting over to Bob*) Don't stand there arguing
with him, can't you see we're losing Nona ...

Bob (*to Jeff*) A convenient double room, was it? With a comfortable double
bed ... ! Once and for all: did you sleep with Terri?

Vera (*going over to Bob and Jeff*) And we don't want any of that sort of
talk, thank you!

*The telephone starts to ring as before: it rings a couple of times before it is
answered by the machine. No-one takes any notice of it*

*Arthur, looking downtrodden and forlorn, enters from the garden carrying a
plastic shopping bag from Boots*

No-one sees him

Lois Mother, just keep out of it. (*To Nona*) Come on, love, cough it up ...

Arthur, unnoticed, points at the ringing telephone

Bob's voice (*from the answering machine*) "Hello, Shotter and Swift. Sorry
we're not here to take your call. Leave your number and we'll ring as soon
as we can. Thanks."

Jeff (*standing and grabbing Bob*) Honestly, Bob, you make me so bloody
angry——

Vera (*protecting Bob*) You dare lay a finger on my son and I'll——

Jeff Just keep out of this—you interfering old cow ... !

Vera I beg your pardon! Lois, did you hear what he just called me?

Lois (*going over to drag Vera away*) Look, Mother, I've told you—just mind
your own business!

Nona sees Arthur and can hardly believe it

Nona (*rushing to Arthur*) Arthur! Oh, thank God—you've come back to
me ...! (*She throws her arms around her husband*) Mum, Lois, Bob—
Arthur's home ... !

Vera, outraged, turns on Arthur now

Vera (*going over to him*) You selfish, no-good, swine and a half—if you think
you can just walk in here and play with my daughter's affections——

Bob (*shouting*) Quiet!

*Sudden silence. A female voice speaks from the machine. Jeff is still holding
Bob, about to hit him, Vera is about to strike Arthur with her bag. Everyone
remains frozen listening to the voice on the telephone*

Female voice (*from the answering machine*) Jeff—are you there? . . . It's me
. . . Terri . . . Hope you and Bob got home safely. Thanks for a lovely time,
Jeff, you really did make my holiday for me. Give me a call later about
next Saturday, you've got the number. Love to you both . . . (*The phone is
put down as she rings off*)

Silence. Everyone looks at everyone else. Jeff sits

Bob (*almost to himself*) The bitch!
Vera So—this Terri's a woman then? (*She sits*)

Everyone now looks at Bob and Jeff

Bob (*quietly*) Yes. This Terri's a woman.

The Lights fade as——

——*the* CURTAIN *falls*

ACT II

The same. Immediately following

The CURTAIN *rises on exactly the same scene as at the end of Act I: Vera, Lois, Nona, Arthur, Bob and Jeff*

Silence

Lois (*breaking the silence*) Come on, Mother, all of you—tea-time!
Vera I want to hear about this young woman.
Lois (*firmly*) Tea-time, Mother! Nona, fetch lover-boy with you.
Nona (*taking Arthur's hand*) You can sit next to me at the table, Arthur.

> *Vera, Lois, Nona and Arthur exit to the kitchen*

Vera (*as she goes*) And I'll carve the capon if you don't mind. It needs an expert!
Lois (*calling to Bob and Jeff*) Come on, boys.

> *Jeff rises, gives Bob a look, then exits*

The Lights fade to a spotlight downstage

Bob (*walking into his light, to the audience*) All right are you? What a life, eh? Who'd have thought that on that perfectly ordinary Saturday afternoon life would have taken such a turn for the worse? (*Sitting on the edge of the stage*) Mind you, that's what you get for going abroad, isn't it? I bet you if we'd gone to Blackpool or Brighton none of this would have happened. It's all that sun—it unbalances the mind. And that bloody awful food. I'll tell you what, I spent the first four days on that toilet. Gippy-tummy, see. And Jeff's always saying he wants to go to Mexico and India. My God, how would I get on there? Montezuma's Revenge or Delhi-Belly I suppose. You're safer at home, aren't you? (*He sighs deeply*)

And did you see me earlier? Making a fool of meself. Behaving like a two year old: spoilt, jealous. But it just goes to show, doesn't it? Go on, admit it: you've done it—we all have.

And what about old Arf turning up, eh? Course you knew he would 'cos we put his name in the programme. Our Lois was right, you see. She said he'd come back, didn't she? Very shrewd is our Lois ... I don't know what we'd do without her to be honest. (*Rising*) Anyway, let's press on, shall we? What about that bitch Terri ringing up? I'll bet you thought she was a fella, too. Not likely. Tell you the truth, I'd have been able to handle it much better if it had been a fella ... but a woman! Well, you feel threatened, don't you?

The Lights come up to full

  Lois enters with a cup of tea for Bob

Bob sits on the stool. Lois joins him

Lois Right, come on then.
Bob Right come on then what?
Lois Are you going to tell me what all this is about?
Bob (*moody again*) Why should I?
Lois Oh, well—please yourself. (*She turns to go*)
Bob (*dejected*) Don't go, Lois. (*Pause*) Talk to me.
Lois Oh, come on, Bob, cheer up. Who's this Terri then?
Bob (*quietly*) They met on a sight-seeing tour in Valetta. So they said. I'd
    stayed back at the apartment—by the pool. I suppose I should have gone
    with him.
Lois Why didn't you?
Bob I thought he might like some breathing space. Time on his own. He
    often leaves me alone to get on with some painting.

Lois sits in the armchair, listening quietly

  Apparently she fell at his feet—literally. She tripped over something in the
  cathedral and grazed her knee. He offered his hanky.
Lois Sounds like a Sunday afternoon film on Channel Four.
Bob The sort you do the ironing to—precisely. The cow. I bet she followed
    him round till she saw an opportunity, then pounced!
Lois He's a very good-looking man, Bob. And he was on his own. I might
    have done the same.
Bob Whose side are you on?
Lois Go on.
Bob It turned out she was on holiday too, staying at an hotel not far from
    us. He brought her back for a cup of tea—and that was that.
Lois There you are then, at least he introduced her.
Bob (*becoming angry*) Introduced her! She was never away. Every single
    day she came round. She'd hired a car and was eager to see as much of the
    island as she could. She had it all planned: guides, maps—a day here, a
    day there. Just up Jeff's street.
Lois And he went with her. Were you invited?
Bob Of course I was. But I always said no, didn't I.
Lois Then it's your fault.
Bob Oh, come off it, Lois, I'd have been the bloody wallflower. She fancied
    him—you could see it in her eyes, in the way she fawned over him.
Lois She never guessed? About you and Jeff?
Bob Obviously not. Fellas do go on holiday together I suppose. But he
    should have told her, shouldn't he?
Lois Don't ask me, love. Perhaps he didn't want to upset her.
Bob A fat lot of help you are. I wouldn't have minded upsetting her.
Lois Then perhaps you should have told her.
Bob I didn't want to upset Jeff, did I.

Lois I see. So Jeff didn't want to upset her, and you didn't want to upset Jeff—now everybody's upset.

Bob She wasn't. Nothing upset her.

Lois (*amused*) But she ruined your holiday. Quite funny really.

Bob There's nothing funny about it, Lois.

Lois Oh, come on, look on the bright side. At least it's all over—you're home.

Bob (*his worst fears*) Is it?

Lois How d'you mean?

Bob You heard her on the phone: "Give me a call". He's even got her phone number.

Lois It happens all the time, love. You meet people on holiday, get on famously for a fortnight, exchange phone numbers—and you never hear from them again.

Bob (*rising*) But we did. The woman phoned here.

Lois A courtesy call—she was being friendly, polite.

Bob Polite my Aunt Fanny. She's after him. I wouldn't be surprised if she turned up on the doorstep.

Pause. He's worried

What's worse ... I think he's after her as well.

Lois Now you're just being daft.

Jeff enters quietly from the kitchen

Bob (*turning to her*) Am I?

He sees Jeff. They look across at each other

Jeff Is he still going on? (*Pause*) Tea's ready. Vera doesn't want to start without "her little son".

Bob exits in silence

Lois You have upset him, haven't you?

Jeff I've upset everybody by the looks of it. Vera won't look at me.

Lois She'll get over it, she usually does.

Jeff She's never really liked me anyway. (*He sits on the sofa*)

Lois You know Mum—she pretends not to like anybody. It's protection against anyone who doesn't like her. That's all. (*She looks at him*)

Jeff (*always at ease with Lois*) It's not all my fault, Lois.

Lois No, I'm sure it isn't—but I only know Bob's side of it.

Jeff I don't know what's come over him, I've never seen him like this before. I thought once his feet were back on English soil he'd give in.

Lois Why should he? You did rather neglect him by the sound of it.

Pause. He doesn't answer

And what's all this about Gozo?

Jeff Oh, God—I can see Gozo's going to haunt me for the rest of my life.

Lois What is it?

Jeff It's a small island. Just off the mainland. Terri and I went there for the day.

Lois You were out with her most days I'm told.

Jeff This was different. We missed the last boat back and got stranded.

Lois All night?

Jeff Yes. Fortunately we found a small guest house.

Lois (*understanding*) Oh dear.

Jeff I can't feel guilty, Lois. I'm sorry. He was at perfect liberty to come with us, but no, he prefers to sit on some godforsaken beach, saturated in sun-oil, painting or reading!

Lois Well, if that makes him happy.

Jeff But it doesn't make me happy, Lois. We went there to sort things out.

Lois What things?

Jeff You know what I'm talking about. Bill must have told you. All I wanted was to discuss things.

Lois You should know my brother by now. He prefers to think that everything's hunky-dory.

Jeff Well, it isn't.

Lois Is that why you picked up this girl?

Jeff No. Of course it isn't. And I did not "pick her up". It was she who spoke first.

Lois You could have ignored her, told her to get lost.

Jeff I could, yes. I even thought about it. But why? We got on well. She was good company. We liked the same things. And, for the life of me, I can't see why it's become such a big deal.

Lois Oh, come on, Jeff, Bob's jealous—he obviously thinks there's more to it.

Pause. No answer

(*Standing*) Well?

Jeff (*with bravado*) If that's what he chooses to think then let him.

Lois You're enjoying all of this, aren't you?

Jeff In a perverse sort of way—yes, I am.

Lois What's she like? Older, younger?

Jeff Hard to say. She's good looking—easy to talk to—intelligent—and an ideal holiday companion. Specially in Malta.

Lois And you were flattered by her attention, is that it?

Jeff All right, if you want the truth, I was flattered. Why not? I haven't been flattered by your brother in years. (*Angry with himself perhaps, he rises*) And don't go on at me, Lois, because I'm trying my hardest not to feel bad about all this.

Silence. She understands him

Lois (*after a while, quietly*) But you do.

Jeff (*quietly*) Yes.

Silence again

Lois Look, you needn't answer if you don't want, but are things that bad between you and Bob?

Jeff Not really. I still love him if that's what you mean.

Lois You're just fed up.

Jeff Bored, Lois. Nothing ever happens.

Lois What d'you want to happen for God's sake? D'you want him to throw things, strike you, find another lover—what?

Jeff I don't know. I just get every day more restless—more irritable.

Lois Does Bob feel the same way?

Jeff Of course he doesn't. He's happy as the day is long.

Lois You know that for sure, do you?

Jeff I can guarantee it. I know your brother like the back of my hand. He loves all this. Everything's "cosy" as he likes to call it. It's "our" home and we've built a life together.

Lois That's nice.

Jeff Oh, I know it's nice. And I can understand how he feels. Apart from his life with Vera he's never known anything else. Let's face it, Lois, he's never been to bed with anyone else. Did you know he was a virgin when I met him?

Lois I didn't, no—but I'm not surprised.

Jeff Why am I telling you all this?

Lois Because I asked.

Jeff You're not embarrassed?

Lois Come off it, why the hell should I be embarrassed?

Jeff I just wondered.

Lois Come on, we'd better go and have our tea. You must be starving.

Jeff I think I'd better stay here—I'll only get a mouthful from Vera.

Lois Oh, come on, I'll stick up for you. You could tell me one thing though.

Jeff What?

Lois I didn't know you were interested in girls.

Jeff Ah, well, you see, you don't know everything.

Lois Obviously not. You, I take it, were not a virgin when you met Bob.

Jeff (*quietly, after a pause*) No. (*Pause*) I had a life before Bob.

Vera (*off, calling*) Lois—are you coming or what?

Lois (*amused*) Come on, into the lion's den.

Jeff What's the betting, the mood she's in, when I walk in she'll walk out.

They both exit to the kitchen. Bob enters DL *and watches them go*

Bob (*to the audience*) I hope you didn't take too much notice of all that. You're supposed to be on my side, remember.

You should see it out there. An atmosphere you could cut with a knife. Me, being moody and refusing to eat; Vera, cutting my chicken up for me as if I were a kid again; Bill, reading the place mats and the label on the sauce bottle; Nona keeps giggling—I think Arthur's twanging her knicker elastic under the table ... Then in walks Lois and Jeff—bold as flaming brass!

Vera storms on from the kitchen followed by Lois

Vera (*upset as usual*) I'm sorry, Lois, I refuse to sit at that table with Jeffrey!

Both come DR

Bob Here we go again . . .

Bob exits DL

Lois Mother, you're getting on my nerves. You're being far too sensitive.

Vera Too sensitive? Too sensitive? Did you say too——

Lois (*cutting in*) Yes, I did. And you're spoiling it for poor Nona. Look how happy she is to have Arthur back.

Vera Oh, everything's all right now is it? Happy endings all round. And what about me?

Lois Have you finished?

Vera No, I haven't. Something's going on here and I want to know what it is. All that rowing upstairs, that shouting out there (*she points to the garden*) and that strange woman with a chap's name—it's not normal, Lois.

Lois Just leave Bob and Jeff to sort their own problems out.

Vera I will not be kept in the dark, I'm that boy's mother.

Lois Shhh, Mother, stop shouting and keep calm.

Vera (*sitting in the* L *armchair*) Don't shush me, Lois. I can't abide being shushed!

Nona and Arthur enter hand in hand from the kitchen

Nona Mother, we can hear you out there. You're upsetting Arthur.

Vera Upsetting who? What's he upset for? It's us who should be upset. He's been gone nearly three weeks with Brenda Fat-face.

Arthur Brenda's not fat. She's got an overactive thyroid, Nona.

Vera She's got an overactive something—I never knew you called it a thyroid!

Lois Don't be coarse, Mother.

Vera Nona, you never did have many brains, even when you were born, but to go and take him back. They should put you away.

Lois Mother, don't take this out on Arthur.

Nona (*a new woman*) Don't worry, Lois. Arthur's strong—he can take it.

Vera Strong? I've seen more attractive lumps in gravy.

Nona It's no use, Mother, insult us all you like. We love each other, don't we, Arthur?

Arthur Which way is the toilet, pet?

Nona Up the stairs, poppet. Second on the left.

Arthur (*as he goes*) Excuse me, Vera, Lois.

Arthur exits upstairs

Nona (*at the stairs, calling after him*) Don't forget to lift the seat, sweetheart. (*To Vera, firmer than before*) Now, what is it, Mother? You're behaving very badly this afternoon. I don't know what Jeff must think.

Vera Who cares what Jeff thinks—balls to Jeff!

Nona (*hand to her mouth with shock*) Mother! Wash your mouth out—this minute!

Vera I'll tell you what, if your dad was alive he'd have a stroke.

Lois He did have, Mother.

Vera Well, he'd have another. (*Standing*) Is this skirt all creased at the back?

Lois (*not even looking*) It looks fine.

Vera And just look at this cardigan—I'm taking it back first thing on Monday. I'd take it back now if I didn't think I'd be missing something. (*She sits on the sofa*)

Lois Come on, Nona, she's all right.

Lois and Nona are about to go back to the kitchen

Jeff enters

Jeff (*quietly to Lois*) How is she? D'you think I should apologize?

Lois That'd be nice—she'll like that.

Vera What does he want?

Lois We'll leave you to it.

Nona Now, don't let her bully you, Jeff.

Lois and Nona exit to the kitchen

Jeff We can't finish our meal without you there, Vera.

Vera Oh, since when have I been that important? I thought I was just an interfering old cow.

Jeff (*almost to himself*) You are—but I shouldn't have said it.

Vera Sorry?

Jeff I said I shouldn't have said it.

Vera It was very hurtful, Jeffrey. After all I've done for you.

Jeff I know—and I'm sorry.

Vera (*calming down*) Yes, well, I'm very easily offended, I know I shouldn't be, but that's my nature.

Jeff (*trying another way*) That's a lovely hat, Vera. Is it new?

Vera I got it half-price in Miami Modes on the market. They had it in royal blue but I thought this would go with anything. (*She looks at him, won over*) Come and sit down, Jeffrey.

He sits beside her on the sofa

Now come on, tell me what's wrong with our Robert. He's not ill, is he? Only you read all sorts in the papers.

Jeff No, Vera, he's not ill. I've just upset him a bit, that's all. It's my fault.

Vera It's to do with that woman on the phone, isn't it?

Jeff In a way—yes, it is.

Vera Don't tell me, I can see it a mile off. Robert's upset that you found a girl-friend and he didn't.

Jeff Perhaps he is, Vera. I never thought of that.

Vera Oh, you can't tell me anything about our Robert. I can read him like a book.

Jeff I know, you're very perspicacious, Vera.

Vera (*in the dark but impressed*) Am I?

Jeff (*rising*) Now, come and finish your tea.

Vera (*pulling him down*) Sit down a minute. I want a word.

Jeff Now, Vera?

Vera It's a day for straight talking, Jeffrey, and I have a few things to say. Now, haven't I always treated you like one of the family?

Jeff (*with another meaning*) You've certainly done that, Vera.

Vera Like a mother almost.

Jeff Yes, Vera.

Vera And you can't say our Robert hasn't been good to you. I mean, he took you into his business.

Jeff I thought we started it together, Vera?

Vera Yes, but with whose money, Jeffrey?

Jeff Yours.

Vera Quite. Not that I begrudge a penny of it, because I don't, but you see what I mean?

Jeff doesn't see what she means but this is no time to argue

He took you under his roof when you were homeless—he brought you here when he moved—he even takes you on holiday with him. There's not many lads would do that, Jeffrey.

Jeff Right.

Vera But it has to be said, and I speak as Robert's mother, I sometimes wonder if you haven't held him back.

Jeff Oh?

Vera Now, please, don't be offended, but has it ever crossed your mind that my son might have been happily married now if it wasn't for you?

Jeff Do you think he might?

Vera He's a very attractive man, Jeffrey. At the height of his prime. (*She looks at him*)

Jeff (*looking at her*) I don't know what to say, Vera.

Vera (*a hand on his knee*) Just think about it, Jeffrey, that's all I want you to do. And just one other thing . . .

Jeff What's that?

Vera This stuff Gozo—I hope it's not a drug.

Jeff No, Vera, it isn't a drug.

Vera Thank God for that. It's only a drink then?

Jeff Sort of.

Arthur has appeared from upstairs and is trying, as if invisible, to sneak to the kitchen without Vera seeing him

Vera Good, like Coca-Cola I expect. (*Suddenly*) Arthur! I want a word with you. Now!

Arthur freezes as if struck by lightning

Off you go. Go and have your tea with Robert—and do try to cheer him up. And tell him not to be jealous—his turn'll come.

Bewildered, Jeff rises and goes back to the kitchen giving Arthur a handshake on the way

(*Adjusting her blouse*) Arthur!

Arthur (*dreading this interview*) Yes, Vera.
Vera Sit down.

He makes towards her to sit beside her

Over there.

He sits in the L armchair

I've just been saying to Jeffrey, it's a day for straight talking, Arthur, and I don't mind admitting you've disappointed me.
Arthur Have I? I thought I might have.
Vera Do you know what it's like to be a mother, Arthur?
Arthur No, Vera, I'm not sure I do.
Vera A mother's like a bird, Arthur. A bird of rare and wondrous plumage. She sits on that nest to protect her eggs until they're hatched.
Arthur (*not sure where all this is leading*) Oh, yes, Vera?
Vera And when those precious little chicks are born, Arthur, that rare and beautiful bird loves those little chicks. Loves, Arthur. She loves them to death. She feeds them, nurtures them, shoves worms and bits of discarded bread down their little throats to keep them alive.
Arthur (*picturing it*) Fancy.
Vera But most of all, she protects those precious chicks. She watches them mature until their feathers are fully grown. And one day, Arthur, her little hen chicks fly off in search of a little cock.
Arthur (*now caught up in this saga*) A little what, Vera?
Vera A man-bird, Arthur. And you know what?
Arthur No. What?
Vera That mother bird is heart-broken. She doesn't show it. She daren't. That would be selfish. But mark my words, she's heart-broken. But as long as she has breath in her body she'll go on protecting her little chicks (*she looks at him*) from buggers like you!
Arthur (*contrite*) I see.
Vera I want an explanation, Arthur.
Arthur I felt in need of a change, Vera. Don't you see?
Vera No, Arthur, I don't see.
Arthur (*hopelessly*) Oh.
Vera Do you remember standing at that altar, Arthur? "To love and to cherish" ... "To have and to hold". The choir? The hymns? That church was freezing and my back was giving me gyp but I smiled through my tears, Arthur. I smiled because it was a holy occasion. My lovely Nona, my first-born remember, was giving herself to you in holy wedlock.

Arthur's head is bent in shame

I am now going into the kitchen to finish my tea, Arthur. I shall leave you here to feel ashamed.

Vera exits to the kitchen, singing

Arthur (*slowly, a thought occurring to him*) But we got married in a registry office! (*He freezes*)

Bob enters DL *as his light comes up*

Bob (*to the audience*) Poor old Arf, eh? You've got to feel a bit sorry for him, haven't you? He'd like to have been on the stage, you know. He would. He can do Elvis Presley . . . Shirley Bassey . . . and you should see his George Formby—quite breathtaking really. He used to have a little ukelele but he sold it to buy Nona a Teasmade. And he's always been a bitter disappointment to Vera. She wanted Nona to marry somebody like Stewart Granger. Except we didn't know anybody like Stewart Granger. But that's Vera for you. She lives in a fantasy world.

The spotlight fades as he joins Arthur

All right, Arf? Don't look so miserable.

Arthur I'm in the dog-house. I knew I would be. Nona's fine, she's welcomed me back with open arms, but Vera won't forget in a hurry.

Bob I'm afraid not. Like elephants, Vera never forgets.

Arthur But I was in need of a change, Bob. You know—a change!

Bob (*sitting on the stool*) Oh, don't you start, Arthur, for God's sake!

Arthur A man has certain needs. He can't go on poking the same fire can he?

Bob (*with deeper meaning*) I thought you had central heating, Arthur.

Arthur What's that supposed to mean?

Bob Nothing, forget I said it.

Bill enters from the kitchen, cheerful as always

Bill Hello, lads. I'm getting out of that lot. Like a bloody wake in there. (*He looks at them*) Christ, doesn't seem much livelier in here.

Arthur I've just had Vera on at me.

Bill Oh, say no more. The Ayatollah hath spoken, eh? Never mind, Arf. You have been a very naughty boy, you know. (*Lowering his voice*) Here, how was big Brenda? You lucky sod, Arf. I've always quite fancied her myself.

Arthur It wasn't quite what I expected, Bill. To tell the truth I was a bit disappointed.

Bill The chase is always more exciting than the conquest, eh Arf?

Arthur Brenda's a very demanding woman, Bill. She gives you no peace, no respite. She'd be at it from breakfast time to supper if she could. She's a chemist, see.

Bill (*after a thought, not knowing what this might imply*) Oh, yeh? (*He sits in the* R *armchair*)

Arthur And she keeps feeding you. Three full meals a day at weekends, coffee at eleven, tea and biscuits at four. I had difficulty lifting anything up.

Bill (*amused*) Poor old Arf, eh, Bob? So you decided to come home, did you?

Arthur And you know what? I got to our front door and she'd only had the bloomin' lock changed. On my front door.

Bill Friggin' sauce! Eh, Bob? Oh, do cheer up, Bob, for Gawd's sake!

Arthur You've been having problems too, have you, Bob?

Bob You could say that.

Arthur Some tart trying to snatch Jeff off you, is that right? I didn't think you and him had women trouble. Old Jeff's not on the change is he? (*He laughs*)

Bob (*rising, moody*) Oh, leave it, Arthur.

Bob exits into the garden

Bill You've got a mouth on you, Arf. See what you've done, you've gone and upset him.

Arthur I didn't mean to. What's it all about?

Bill Wouldn't know, Arf. Keep out of it, that's my motto.

Arthur Nobody's immune you see. But I must say I'm surprised. I thought things were different when you were bent.

Silence. Arthur is deep in thought

You know, Bill, I wouldn't say this to anyone else so keep it under your hat. I've often thought I might like to be gay.

Bill Jesus, Arf, that'd put a stop to it—knock it right on the head that would.

Arthur (*offended*) Here, what d'you mean?

Nona enters from the kitchen with a cup of tea in her hand

Nona Arthur, I'm missing you out there.

Arthur Hello, treasure pot. I was just having a man-to-man with Bill here.

Bill You wanna keep an eye on him, Nona.

Nona (*sitting on Arthur's knee*) I will, don't you worry. Oh, I am glad you're back, Arthur. Life can get back to normal. Why did you go, why did you break my heart like that?

Arthur (*embarrassed*) Not in front of Bill, Nona, please.

Nona Bill doesn't mind, do you, Bill?

Bill (*engrossed in his paper*) What?

Nona I don't hate Brenda Brierley, Arthur.

Arthur Don't you? I do.

Nona I don't hate her because I can understand. She saw in you all the endearing qualities that I so admire.

Bill Leave it out, Nona. You're turning my stomach here.

Nona And you'll see, pet. I'm going to make a big effort. Our marriage will be stronger from henceforth on. (*Holding up her cup*) I've started having sugar in my tea—to put on some weight, see.

Arthur Very nice.

The peace is again disturbed by Lois, in determined mood, dragging in Jeff from the kitchen

Jeff Leave it, Lois, if he doesn't want to see reason——

Lois No, Jeff, we've got to settle this now. We've had enough bloody misery with Nona since Arthur's been away.

Bill What the hell's going on now?

Lois Where's Bob?
Bill In the garden.
Lois Still sulking?
Bill I expect so. Old Arf upset him. (*Rising to get out of all this*) Shall I get him?
Lois Stay where you are.
Bill Are you ordering me about or what?
Lois Yes.

Bill sits on the sofa

Right, now I want everybody to make an effort.
Nona (*smiling*) That's just what I've said to Arthur.
Lois Just keep quiet, Nona.
Nona (*standing*) Arthur, are you going to allow her to speak to me like that?
Arthur (*rising to protest*) Now, look here, Lois——
Lois Oh, sit down, Arthur, you're going to need all your energy for when you get home.

Arthur sits on the sofa

Nona (*to Arthur*) What does she mean by that? (*She sits on the sofa arm*)
Lois (*ignoring all this*) Well, Jeff?
Jeff This is embarrassing, Lois. We don't want all this fuss.
Lois Oh, yes we do. We've sorted out Nona and Arthur this afternoon, we can sort you and Bob out as well. You could go on like this for weeks. Now, why don't you tell us, what did you get up to on Gozo?
Nona It's none of our business, Lois.
Lois I don't agree. It's Bob's business and what affects Bob affects us, Nona. You men, you're all the bloody same. Just because you get fed up and fancy a change you think you can just sod off—have it away with peroxide blondes from Boots or (*looking at Jeff*) wherever else happens to be handy, then come home whenever it suits you and expect everything to be normal.
Nona Are you referring to my Arthur? Arthur, is she referring to you?
Lois I'm generalizing, Nona, generalizing, dear.
Nona Oh, that's all right then. (*To Arthur*) She's generalizing.
Lois Now, Jeff, we're supposed to be a family here, so why don't you just come out with it and tell us what's bothering you?

Everyone looks at Jeff

Jeff (*feeling cornered*) Nothing's bothering me. It's your brother out there.
Lois He's upset about what happened in Malta. I'm concerned about what's happening here in this house.
Jeff Now, hang on, Lois, I don't have to take any of this from you. (*He sits on the stool*)

Vera enters from the kitchen

Vera What's all this now? What am I missing?
Lois Jeff's just about to tell us something. Go on, Jeff.

Jeff (*cornered, uncomfortable*) How can I, Lois? In front of Vera.
Vera Why, what have I done?
Lois (*firmly*) Mother, either shut up or shift!

Vera is open-mouthed, about to protest. She sits in the R armchair

Now, Jeff, we're listening. (*She sits in the L armchair*)

Lois' ploy to get the truth out of Jeff seems to be working: it's crunch time for Jeff, he takes a deep breath

Jeff (*at length, trapped*) All right then ... yes, I do have something to say ... I do have a problem ... but it's my problem and it concerns only Bob.
Lois I've told you once already—we're a family here, Jeff. What concerns Bob concerns us all.
Jeff You're not my family, Lois. I haven't got a family, have I?
Lois What are we? Scotch mist?
Jeff You know what I mean, Lois. I haven't a family of my own. And suddenly—perhaps since my mum died—it's started to bother me. I feel so bloody alone.
Vera I know what he means.

They all look at her

I can get very lonely—stuck in that house on my own.
Jeff (*knowing she means well*) I didn't say I was lonely, Vera. I'm not lonely. I said I feel alone.

Pause. They all listen

After my mum died last year—and, please, I don't want you feeling sorry for me—but when she died and I sat there, in that hospital, holding her hand—I suddenly realized. There was only ever the two of us. I had no brothers, no sisters, and because I never knew who my father was I wasn't even sure if I had any relations at all. I may have, I suppose—but where are they? Who are they? (*Pause*) Well, I can live with that, I can come to terms with it. In fact, sometimes when I see you lot having a row, I think I'm better off!
Vera (*offended*) I'm sorry, but——

Bob enters unnoticed from the garden

Lois Mother!
Jeff (*unaware of these interruptions*) But what I'm finding difficult to live with—what I can't come to terms with—is that I'm nobody's father. (*Simply*) Is that silly?
Lois (*with great understanding*) No, it isn't silly at all.
Jeff I just wish I had kids, that's all. Like you and Bill. I mean, at least my mum had me, didn't she. But who have I got? Who's going to succeed me? Who?

Silence. No-one has an answer

It's probably pure selfishness, I don't know, but I cannot shift it from my mind. It follows me around—everywhere.

Silence

Bob (*after the pause*) Oh?

They all turn to see Bob. Silence

(*Quietly*) I'd like a word with Jeff. In private, please.

Everyone rises to go except Vera

You too, Mum.

They all exit leaving Bob and Jeff alone

The following scene is played slowly and quietly

(*After a while*) Well?

Jeff (*not looking at him*) Well?

Bob What was all that about?

Jeff I'm sorry.

Pause

Bob Why haven't you ever told me any of that?

Jeff You know why. Because it sounded like carping. Because it came out sounding as futile, as silly, and as trivial as I feared it would.

Bob It didn't sound futile. Or trivial. It sounded quite sincere and genuine. That's what worries me. (*He comes and sits on the arm of the chair near Jeff*)

Jeff There's no need to be nice to me. I realize I've upset you.

Silence. Bob looks at Jeff who refuses to look at him

Bob (*calm, quiet*) You must admit it would be better if this sort of thing was kept private. Just between ourselves. Instead of being blurted out in front of the entire family. (*Pause*) But then I gather I've become impossible to talk to. (*Pause*) I'd foolishly led myself to believe that we could tell each other anything. That isn't so then?

Jeff Perhaps not. Look, maybe I've got everything out of proportion. Maybe—because of the uneventful life we lead, because we live as we do—maybe I have too much time to think.

Bob I have just as much time.

Jeff Yes, but you seem able to occupy it differently to me.

Bob Meaning?

Jeff (*turning to him*) You know what I mean, Bob. You're content to watch television all night. Paint if you wish. You always seem to be doing something.

Now Bob has turned away

Bob So?

Jeff I'm different that's all. I'm more thoughtful, more introspective I suppose.

Bob I'm not as intelligent as you, is that what you're trying to say?

Jeff No.

Bob First I'm naïve, now I'm thick.

Jeff I'm not saying that. If you must know I envy you. You never seem to worry, you're seldom in a mood, you're always cheerful—and of course that's what I love about you, that's what everybody loves about you.

Bob You'd prefer me to be bloody miserable all day, is that it?

Jeff looks at him with impatience

Then say what you mean, Jeff.

Jeff (*trying hard to explain*) Look, I'm a solitary person——

Bob Oh, here we go ...

Jeff Just listen, will you——?

Bob (*more forcefully now*) Ever since I can remember you've been saying that. As long as we've been together you've been saying it.

Jeff Well, it's a fact!

Bob All right, so it's a fact. Except you hold it up as some sort of virtue—a gift from God that's been denied the rest of us. We could all be solitary if we wanted, but we live in this world, Jeff, not on flippin' Mars! We have to meet people—especially in our job—meet them, be nice to them, smile, be charming. If you're that solitary you should go and live on your own, in the middle of a bloody field!

Silence. Bob is sorry he lost his temper

(*Gentler now*) And what's all this about kids?

Jeff Never mind, it's not important.

Bob I'm asking.

Jeff And I've answered—it's not important.

Bob (*sarcastic*) Why not give Terri a ring, I'm sure she'll listen.

Jeff (*losing his temper; standing and moving to the sofa*) She has listened, she's spent the last fortnight listening. At least she understood. I miss not having children that's all—is that so terrible?

Bob Only because you make it sound so terrible. There must be millions of married couples who can't have children. Look at Nona and Arthur: they haven't any kids.

Jeff Look at Lois and Bill: they've got a bloody houseful.

Bob Well, have a word with them. Go on, if you ask nicely they might even give you one.

Jeff Don't talk bollocks! (*He sits on the sofa*)

Bob (*rising*) Look, Jeff I don't see the problem. You can have kids if you want them, you're not impotent. Find a woman, have a child—have half a dozen. But I'll tell you one thing, you'll still be solitary as you call it, because that's the way you are. (*Anger again*) So stop feeling so bloody sorry for yourself!

Silence. The two men look at each other then Jeff turns away. Bob's light comes up DR *as he walks into it and addresses the audience*

(*Annoyed with himself but always good humoured*) Shit! I shouldn't have said all that, should I? (*He sighs*) Well, I am trying to understand. Go on, admit it, you feel sorry for him and not me. I knew it! Would you credit it!

You can see what's happening, can't you? This is turning into a bloody Greek tragedy with him as the doomed hero and me as the poor sod who gets his eyes gouged out and his balls cut off! (*Needing to defend himself*) Well, at least I know what I am, and it's never bothered me.

It's not my fault if Jeff's having some sort of identity crisis, is it? That's what's happening. He knows what his preferences are but he's beginning to wonder whether it wouldn't have been better to stick to the straight and narrow.

Well, what am I supposed to say to him?

Pause

I can remember my dad once saying, "Some folk are born one way, some another, and some are lucky enough to be born both ways". I never knew what he meant—but I'm beginning to. Except I wouldn't call it lucky, would you? Not if it throws you into turmoil.

He is about to turn to go back to Jeff, but stops

Hang on, there's worse to come. Pretend you're not here. (*He moves back into the scene*)

The Lights return to normal

Lois enters from the kitchen on her way upstairs. She stops and looks at Bob and Jeff

(*To Lois*) Look, sod off, will you. We are trying to have a private conversation here!

Lois goes upstairs and exits

Bob quietly sits at Jeff's feet and the scene continues

(*Quieter now*) Look, I am trying to understand, Jeff. (*Pause*) How long have you felt like this?
Jeff Since Mum died.
Bob I see. And there was me thinking you'd taken it pretty well.
Jeff I don't tell you everything.
Bob No, that's what this is all about. Perhaps it's time you started. (*Pause. He looks up at his friend*) Come on, there's something else, isn't there?

No reply

What?
Jeff (*finding it difficult*) The girl I used to know, remember? Before I met you.
Bob (*uneasy*) I don't want to know about it, Jeff. We agreed to forget all about that.
Jeff I know, and I'm sorry, but it's important. I can't stop thinking about her.

Pause. Jeff looks at Bob who is looking down at his shoes unhappy with all this

You see, there's one thing I never told you. (*Pause*) She had a baby. My baby. A girl.

Bob is badly affected. He attempts to get to his feet but Jeff restrains him by putting a hand on his sho:.lder

No, listen. Please. I never saw the baby. But I keep wondering what she looks like now. Wondering where she is. Could I pass her in the street? Sit opposite her in a train? Asking myself would I know her. Would she know me.

Pause

So you see, I do have a family somewhere—a daughter at least. And sometimes, usually at night, when you're in there watching the telly, or when I'm out jogging . . . I miss her.

Bob (*at length, quietly*) Thank you for telling me.

Jeff Are you all right?

Bob (*taking his hand*) I'm fine.

They smile at each other

What're we going to do?

Jeff I don't know. I'm lost.

Bob Is this why you took Terri's phone number, because you want to see her again?

Jeff I'm not sure. I know she wants to see me again.

Bob is silent

She is nice, Bob. Just like us really. On the surface she appears to have everything, but she's unhappy—lonely.

Bob Did you tell her about us?

Jeff (*knowing it will hurt*) No. I'm sorry. Don't ask me why—pride I expect—it gave me some sort of kick, pretending to be normal.

Bob You once told me we were normal.

Jeff We are. We are normal . . . except . . .

Bob (*looking at him*) Except we're not. (*He rises in silence. Not looking at his friend*) I can't stop you going away, Jeff. If that's what you want.

Pause. No answer

(*It has to be asked*) Did anything happen? That night?

Jeff We did have a double room. And a double bed. But nothing happened.

Bob turns to him hopefully

But it could have done.

Bob (*hurt*) Couldn't she see we were a couple? Isn't it obvious?

Jeff People only see what they want to see. Look at our customers, it never crosses their minds. Look at Vera, she's a prime example. If it should be obvious to anyone it's her.

Bob I know. I've often thought that if we split up Mum would think you were simply moving on.

Jeff Yes. Sad, isn't it?

Lois comes down the stairs and stops halfway

Lois That cat's fretting up there—he's upset and sick of being ignored.
Bob What's he upset for? He's got the life of Old Riley.
Lois He's wondering if he's going to be the victim of a broken home. (*She comes downstairs*)
Bob (*trying to lighten the mood*) At least he's been "seen to". (*To Jeff*) Perhaps I should get you done!
Jeff (*rising and going upstairs*) That'd be no good to you! I'll be upstairs with the cat if I'm needed.

Jeff exits upstairs

Lois (*eager to know the outcome*) Well?
Bob You're a nosey bugger, you, our Lois. This was all your doing, wasn't it?
Lois Bringing matters to a head? Yes. It had to be done, Bob.
Bob Had it? I was quite happy with things as they were.
Lois Oh, come on, you're beginning to sound like Vera.
Bob What's that supposed to mean?
Lois You've got to face up to things, love. It's no use keeping somebody caged if they want to be free. Look at Dad. It killed him in the finish. Pretending to be what he wasn't.
Bob (*after a pause, puzzled*) Dad?
Lois Did you never put two and two together? He longed to be out of it.
Bob But Mum's always said he never even looked at another woman.
Lois That's true. I don't think he ever looked at another woman, love.

Long pause. He tries to take it in

Bob Does Bill know all this? Nona?
Lois Course they don't. I've never discussed it before.
Bob Did Mum understand?
Lois Who knows what Mum understands—she'd rather pretend nothing's happening.
Bob Like me?
Lois We're all made the way we are, love. You'll never change that. All I'm saying is that if Jeff wants to go, you must let him. (*Pause*) Does he?
Bob (*quietly*) I'm not sure. (*Pause*) But whatever he decides . . . I won't stop him, Lois.
Lois (*smiling*) Good. I'm proud of you.

Lois exits to the kitchen

Bob is left alone. Deep in thought he stares out into the middle distance. Maybe, just for a brief moment, it seems he is going to speak but suddenly the telephone starts to ring. As before it rings a couple of times and is answered by the machine

Bob's voice (*from the machine*) "Hello, Shotter and Swift. Sorry we're not here to take your call. Leave your number and we'll ring as soon as we can. Thanks." (*There is a bleep from the machine*)

Jeff comes quickly downstairs

He looks across at Bob as they listen to the message

Female voice (*from the machine*) "Jeff? It's me again—Terri. Are you there?

Bob quickly crosses to the phone and looks down at it

I'm sorry to ring again but I'm getting a bit anxious. I hope you're back safely . . . ?

Bob, trying not to show how upset he really is, exits to the garden

It's just that I found your sunglasses. They were behind the seat when I handed the car back in Malta.

Jeff goes to the phone and is about to pick it up but something stops him

Oh, well—you're obviously not there. Never mind. I might see you. I might not." (*Pause, then she rings off*)

Jeff looks at the phone, then out to the garden where Bob has gone. It seems as if he might be about to go out there

Too late. *The moment is shattered by the entrance of Vera, Lois, Nona, Bill and Arthur*

Vera Well, I can't sit round here all day. I can see I'm not wanted anyway. Bill, get this mother-to-be home.

Bill Thank God for that, I've been wanting to go since I came. (*He puts on his jacket*)

Vera I suppose you'll be seeing Doris tonight. That should make you happy, I know you all get on better with her than you do with me.

Bill We do actually, Vera, yes.

Lois Bill, don't start.

Vera And Nona, now I'm warning you: keep your eyes on him, otherwise he'll be off again. Bugger! (*Looking round*) Where's our Robert?

Jeff In the garden.

Vera Still got a mood on him I expect. Right, come on, you lot. Bill, you'll give Nona and Arthur a lift.

Bill Oh, yes, Bill's taxi service. Are you coming, Vera? You could say hello to the kids.

Vera I suppose Doris'll be there as usual.

Bill Of course.

Vera No thanks, I'd sooner walk.

Bill (*turning to go*) Please yourself. Bye, Jeff.

Jeff Bye, Bill, and thanks for the lift.

Bill You're welcome, lad, anytime.

Bill exits

Lois (*kissing Vera*) Bye, Mum. Shall we see you tomorrow for tea or what?

Vera You might, you never know—depends how I feel.

Nona (*kissing Vera*) Bye, Mum. I'm over the moon about Arthur.

Vera You've always been halfway over the moon, Nona.

Arthur Goodbye, Vera.

Vera And think on, Arthur—that little mother bird, remember.

Arthur (*kissing Vera*) Don't worry, Vera. I shan't be going anywhere near Boots.

Jeff I'll see you out.

One by one they all exit leaving the stage empty. Bob enters DL

A spotlight comes up on him DL

Bob (*to the audience*) I feel a right twat, don't I? A right prick'n' a half.

All that about me dad . . . who'd have thought, eh? (*Warning*) And don't go telling anybody—right! It's private.

They've all just buggered off. Left me here on my own. They'll be chopping down the sodding cherry trees next!

As if this might be surprising

Oh, we do go to the theatre you know, we're not ignorant! Think it's over do you? Well, it's not, see—so you can stop putting your shoes on and eating your last Black Magic.

Vera comes back from the street singing to herself. She goes to the mirror

Vera (*singing*) "Love walked right in, and drove the shadows away—love walked right in and brought my sunniest day . . ." (*Seeing Bob*) Oh, so you've decided to come in, have you?

Bob (*to the audience, not what he expected*) What?

Vera (*tidying up, etc., not looking at him*) I suppose you know they've all gone—left. They asked after you, but I said: "Oh, leave him," I said, "let him sulk", I said.

Bob (*to the audience*) I don't believe this, do you?

Vera (*still busy, not looking at him*) The trouble with you, our Robert, you've been spoilt. Wait till you get married. No wife will put up with this, you know. I'm your mother—mothers are different, mothers understand. You've behaved very badly this afternoon. All that shouting at Jeff, I was ashamed I can tell you. (*She sits in the armchair*)

The spotlight fades

Bob (*to Vera*) What're you on about?

Vera And that poor lad—breaking down like that. My heart bled for him. You couldn't care less, I suppose. (*She powders her nose*)

Bob (*astounded*) You what!

Vera It's all right for you, Robert, you've never gone short of love, but that lad's been starved of it. Never mind, that Terri'll soon put that right.

Bob Oh, will she—you know that, do you? (*He sits on the sofa*)

Vera I've never met her, but I can tell she's a bit like me: a heart of pure gold—you could hear it in her voice, and I'm not easily fooled. Ask me, they'll be married and out of it within the year. They fell in love in Malta, I dare say. "Malta, Isle of Love"—isn't there a song called that?

Bob You're turning my stomach here, Mother.
Vera Don't be sarcastic. You're not too old to have your hands and face smacked, young man.
Bob (*to the audience*) I give up.
Vera Can't you see I worry about you, Robert? If you're not careful Jeffrey'll be off, happy as Larry, and where will you be then? On the shelf with the teapot.

Bob just rolls his eyes to heaven and starts reading the paper Bill left. Vera joins Bob on the sofa

Why don't you find a nice young woman, Robert? Smart, well set up, clever? Look at Sylvia Twine. You loved that little girl in her nice white ballet frock.
Bob Mother——
Vera Let me finish, will you . . . Look at Sylvia now . . . she's ever so big in the Halifax—her own till and everything—and every time I go in she asks after you.
Bob She's married, Mother. Sylvia Twine is married!
Vera She's not happy, you can see it written all over her face. And have you seen her husband? No, you'd have been on Happy Street now if you'd married Sylvia.
Bob You're depressing me, Mother.
Vera (*rising*) When I'm dead and gone you'll be thanking me. (*Looking around*) Now, where did I put me bag?
Bob You're not actually going?
Vera I can't hang around here all day, Robert. There's others beside you who call for my attention. I've got to visit Trish this evening. I'll be losing her next.
Bob Why, where's she going?
Vera You know very well where she's going—you're like our Lois and Nona, you, you never listen to a word I say. My sister's on her last legs, if you must know, and I'm not far behind—that'll solve all your problems. (*Adjusting her clothing*) How do I look? (*At the mirror*)

Pause. She resets her hat then turns and looks at him. She smiles as mothers do and goes over to him, arms outstretched. Bob stands and Vera joins him c

Still—you're my little son, aren't you. (*She tries to encase him*)
Bob (*shrugging her off*) Gerroff!
Vera Oh, cheer up, Robert. If I didn't tell you off now and again who would? Look on the bright side, be like me, always optimistic: remember the doughnut and the hole?
Bob The what?
Vera Your dad, bless him, he used to say, "Vera", he'd say "you're the eternal optimist, you only ever see the doughnut, whereas me, I only see the hole!"
Bob (*to the audience*) This is what I have to put up with.
Vera Who're you talking to?
Bob Nobody.

Vera Well, must be off. I'll be round next week if I'm still here. I've seen a
   lovely jumper for you in Marks, paradise blue, I'll get it for you as a
   treat—cheer you up a bit. (*She looks at him*) Well, don't I get a kiss?

He kisses her. She makes to go

   And remember what I've said.
Bob (*now or never*) Mum?
Vera (*stopping at the door*) Yes, son?

Pause. She looks over at him but he hasn't turned to her

Bob (*with great difficulty*) Mum.
Vera What, Robert?

Pause

Bob Is there anything you want to ask me?
Vera Ask you?
Bob Yes. Ask me.
Vera No. (*Pause*) I don't think so.

*Silence. Vera is cleverer perhaps than she has appeared so far. She looks
across at her son*

   Why? Is there anything you want to tell me?

Long pause. He slowly turns to look at her

Bob (*smiling*) No.

The Lights start to fade slowly

   Vera exits

Bob moves L and a pool of light comes up on him

   (*To the audience*) You see what I mean about telling lies? There is
   something I want to tell her, and she's got something to ask me ... but,
   well ... there it is.

*Jeff comes jogging on, dressed as he was at the beginning of the play in his
shorts and vest*

Bob watches him for a while

   He's here: Jogging Jeffrey Shotter.

Jeff sinks on to the sofa, exhausted

Jeff (*breathless*) Jesus! I'm knackered!
Bob (*to the audience*) You know the routine: "What's for tea?" (*He joins the
   scene*)
Jeff (*unaware of the audience*) What's for tea?
Bob "Kippers and custard and see if you like it!"
Jeff (*looking over at him, pulling a face*) Kippers and custard—that's
   disgusting!

Bob (*to the audience*) My God, he's actually listening. (*He sits on the sofa*)
Jeff (*rising*) You know, sometimes I think you live in a world of your own.
  (*He takes an apple from the bowl on the table and turns to leave the room*)
Bob Jeff . . . ?
Jeff (*stopping, turning*) Bob?
Bob You would warn me, wouldn't you?
Jeff (*puzzled*) Warn you? About what?
Bob If you felt like going to go to Gozo again?

Jeff, about to bite into the apple, pauses, then throws the apple over to Bob and gets himself another. They look across the room at each other, then cheerfully each one bites into his apple

The Lights slowly fade as——

—*the* CURTAIN *falls*

FURNITURE AND PROPERTY LIST

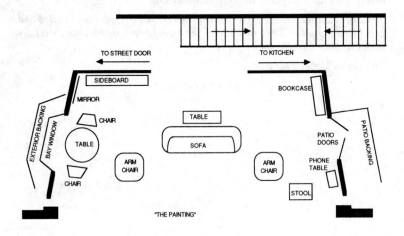

ACT I

On stage: Sideboard
   Bookcase. *On shelves*: books
   Table. *On it*: bowl containing apples
   2 chairs
   Sofa table. *On it*: magazine
   Sofa. *On it*: cushions
   2 armchairs
   Stool
   Small table. *On it*: telephone, answering-machine, watering can
   Mirror on wall
   Paintings on wall by stairs
   Patio doors closed
   Curtains open at window

Off stage: Can of drink **(Jeff)**
   Bags of shopping, containing various items including a box of Go-Cat and
      packet of tissues **(Nona)**
   Bags of shopping **(Lois)**
   Shopping bag containing aerosol can, foil-wrapped chicken, knitting;
      handbag containing powder compact **(Vera)**
   Raw carrot, invoices **(Jeff)**
   Mixing bowl, wooden spoon **(Bob)**
   Bag of apples **(Vera)**

Saucer **(Lois)**
Apple **(Jeff)**
"Air Malta" bag, artist's folding easel **(Bob)**
Suitcases **(Bill)**
Boots plastic carrier bag **(Arthur)**

Personal: **Lois:** packet of cigarettes, lighter
Nona: wrist-watch, handkerchief
Bill: newspaper in jacket pocket

ACT II

On stage: As before

Off stage: Cup of tea **(Lois)**
Cup of tea **(Nona)**

LIGHTING PLOT

Property fittings required: nil

Interior. The same scene throughout

ACT I

To open: Black-out

Cue 1	When ready *Bring up spot on* **Bob** DL	(Page 1)
Cue 2	**Bob**: "... but it never is." *Gradually bring up lighting to half overall*	(Page 2)
Cue 3	**Jeff** exits *Increase lighting to full with warm afternoon sunshine effect through window and patio doors*	(Page 3)
Cue 4	At the end of the answering-machine message *Reduce lighting slightly to indicate time change*	(Page 7)
Cue 5	**Bob**: "... more about that later." *Return to previous level*	(Page 8)
Cue 6	**Bob**: "Ages ago, Lois said she must know ..." *Reduce lighting slightly to indicate time change*	(Page 13)
Cue 7	**Bob**: "Am I?" *Reduce lighting slightly more to indicate time change*	(Page 14)
Cue 8	**Bob**: "We went through a bad patch and ..." *Increase lighting to full with warm afternoon sunshine effect through windows and patio doors*	(Page 15)
Cue 9	**Bill** goes back to his paper *Reduce lighting overall but increase lighting on* **Bill** *and bring up spot on* **Bob** DL	(Page 19)
Cue 10	**Bob**: "... it seems, sometime back ..." *Cross-fade to subdued overall lighting*	(Page 19)
Cue 11	**Bill**: "... cooling down, mate!" *Snap on full general lighting as before*	(Page 22)
Cue 12	**Bob**: "This Terri's a woman." *Slow fade to black-out*	(Page 28)

ACT II

To open: Full general lighting with warm afternoon sunshine effect
through window and patio doors

Cue 13   **Jeff** exits   (Page 29)
            Fade to spot downstage

Cue 14   **Bob**: "Well, you feel threatened, don't you?"   (Page 29)
            Bring up full general lighting as before

Cue 15   **Arthur**: "But we got married in a registry office!"   (Page 37)
            Reduce lighting overall, bring up spot DL

Cue 16   **Bob**: "She lives in a fantasy world."   (Page 38)
            Return lighting to previous level, fade spot

Cue 17   **Jeff** turns away   (Page 43)
            Reduce lighting overall, bring up spot DR

Cue 18   **Bob**: "Pretend you're not here."   (Page 44)
            Return to previous level, fade spot

Cue 19   **Bob** enters DL   (Page 48)
            Spot DL *on* **Bob**

Cue 20   **Vera** sits   (Page 48)
            Fade spot

Cue 21   **Bob**: "No."   (Page 50)
            Start slow fade

Cue 22   **Bob** moves L   (Page 50)
            Bring up pool of light on **Bob** L

Cue 23   Each one bites into his apple   (Page 51)
            Slow fade to black-out

EFFECTS PLOT

ACT I

Cue 1   **Bob**: "... at the airport."   (Page 7)
Telephone rings twice; then answering machine as script page 7

Cue 2   **Vera**: "... still here at Christmas."   (Page 17)
Car pulls up outside

Cue 3   **Vera**: "... that sort of talk, thank you!"   (Page 27)
Telephone rings twice; then answering-machine as script pages 27–28

ACT II

Cue 4   **Bob** seems as if he is going to speak   (Page 46)
Telephone rings twice; then answering-machine as script pages 46–47

MADE AND PRINTED IN GREAT BRITAIN BY
LATIMER TREND & COMPANY LTD PLYMOUTH

MADE IN ENGLAND